ASHES TO DUST

GRAHAM COOKSON

www.knowthescorebooks.com

KNOW THE SCORE BOOKS PUBLICATIONS

CULT HEROES	Author	ISBN
CHELSEA	Leo Moynihan	1-905449-00-3
MANCHESTER CITY	David Clayton	978-1-905449-05-7
NEWCASTLE	Dylan Younger	1-905449-03-8
SOUTHAMPTON	Jeremy WIson	1-905449-01-1
WEST BROM	Simon Wight	1-905449-02-X

MATCH OF MY LIFE	Editor	ISBN
ENGLAND WORLD CUP	Massarella & Moynihan	1-905449-52-6
EUROPEAN CUP FINALS	Ben Lyttleton	1-905449-57-7
FA CUP FINALS 1953-1969	David Saffer	978-1-905449-53-8
FULHAM	Michael Heatley	1-905449-51-8
LEEDS	David Saffer	1-905449-54-2
LIVERPOOL	Leo Moynihan	1-905449-50-X
SHEFFIELD UNITED	Nick Johnson	1-905449-62-3
STOKE CITY	Simon Lowe	978-1-905449-55-2
SUNDERLAND	Rob Mason	1-905449-60-7
SPURS	Allen & Massarella	978-1-905449-58-3
WOLVES	Simon Lowe	1-905449-56-9

GENERAL FOOTBALL	Author	ISBN
BURKSEY	Peter Morfoot	1-905449-49-6
TACKLES LIKE A FERRET	Paul Parker	1-905449-47-X
WORLD CUP DIARY	Harry Harris	1-905449-90-9
HOLD THE BACK PAGE	Harry Harris	1-905449-91-7

CRICKET	Author	ISBN
ASHES TO DUST	Graham Cookson	978-1-905449-19-4
GROVEL!	David Tossell	978-1-905449-43-9
MOML: THE ASHES	Pilger & Wightman	1-905449-63-1
WASTED?	Paul Smith	978-1-905449-45-3

FORTHCOMING PUBLICATIONS IN 2007

CULT HEROES	Author	ISBN
CARLISLE UNITED	Mark Harrison	978-1-905449-09-7
CELTIC	David Potter	978-1-905449-08-8
NOTTINGHAM FOREST	David McVay	978-1-905449-06-4
RANGERS	Paul Smith	978-1-905449-07-1

MATCH OF MY LIFE	Editor	ISBN
ASTON VILLA	Neil Moxley	978-1-905449-65-1
BOLTON WANDERERS	David Saffer	978-1-905449-64-4
DERBY COUNTY	Johnson & Matthews	978-1-905449-68-2
MANCHESTER UNITED	Brian Hughes	978-1-905449-59-0

GENERAL FOOTBALL	Author	ISBN
CHAMPIONS LEAGUE YEARBOOK	Harry Harris	978-1-905449-93-4
OUTCASTS The Lands FIFA Forgot	Steve Menary	978-1-905449-31-6
PARISH TO PLANET	Dr Eric Midwinter	978-1-905449-30-9
MY PREMIERSHIP DIARY	Marcus Hahnemann	978-1-905449-33-0

CRICKET	Author	ISBN
MY TURN TO SPIN	Shaun Udal	978-1-905449-42-2
LEAGUE CRICKET YEARBOOK North West edition	Andy Searle	978-1-905449-70-5
LEAGUE CRICKET YEARBOOK North East edition	Andy Searle	978-1-905449-71-2
LEAGUE CRICKET YEARBOOK Midlands edition	Andy Searle	978-1-905449-72-9

ASHES TO DUST

GRAHAM COOKSON

www.knowthescorebooks.com

First published in the United Kingdom
by Know The Score Books Limited, 2007

Know The Score Books Limited
118 Alcester Road, Studley, Warwickshire, B80 7NT
Tel: 01527 454482   Fax: 01527 452183
info@knowthescorebooks.com

www.knowthescorebooks.com

A CIP catalogue record is available for this book from the British Library
ISBN: 978-1-905449-19-4

Jacket and book design by Simon Lowe

Printed and bound in Great Britain
By Cromwell Press, Trowbridge, Wiltshire

Mixed Sources
Product group from well-managed
forests and other controlled sources
www.fsc.org Cert no. TT-TOC-2082
© 1996 Forest Stewardship Council
FSC

Front cover:

England fans show yet more of that famous Dunkirk spirit as the team capitulate on the final day in Brisbane.

Rear cover (in descending order)

Pic 1 – Dangerously near Barmy Army Jimmy's armpit at Adelaide

Pic 2 – In Perth where Monty finally got the thumbs up

Pic 3 – Some of the more soberly dressed Aussies in Brisbane

Pic 4 – He's a celebrity... get me out of here!

Acknowledgements

A big thank you to: -

Deborah Cookson, Kate Dalby, John Ruane and Barrie Stoddard, four top people who have not only assisted with the book, but also helped me when it's really mattered.

The people who have given me the breaks and the confidence to do this kind of thing; Colin Bower, Liza Brown, Suzanne Case, Katy Cooke, Heidi Dawson, Chris Hargrave, Simon Lowe, Andy Lulham, Mark O'Brien, Lindsey Rosser, Andy Searle, Kevin Trotter, Eleanor Walsh and David and Martin at Real Life News. If I've forgotten any-one, sorry, I'll get you next time promise.

Matthew Shackleton, who deserves a worthy mention for his pics and company in Australia, as does Chris Hargreaves and all the people who follow the England cricket team overseas.

My friends and comrades in the Fylde Coast, Merseyside and West Yorkshire areas, for helping give me a weird sense of humour and the belief that it's important to always try to be funny.

The temptation is to finish (like people used to on Radio One) by saying 'and anyone else who knows me.' But that's rubbish, some of them are horrible.

So thanks to anyone else who likes me.

INDEX

To Mum, Dad, Deb and Mol

(P.S. Ignore the swearing; we all know I'd never really use those kind of words)

Foreword

It is amazing to look back on the first tour of Australia that I went on in 1994, aged 27. I was realising my lifelong dream of watching the Ashes Down Under. From an early age I had loved watching and playing cricket and then to be there watching this incredible series live was amazing. Very much like watching football in England, there was a greater buzz travelling away from home and for the vast majority of cricket fans the Ashes in Australia was and always will be the pinnacle of their ambition, it is the ultimate sporting series.

Arriving at The GABBA in November '94 there was never a plan to start the Barmy Army, it just evolved, England were playing badly, the home crowd were baiting us incessantly and the loose collection of travelling fans grouped by the old tea bar were looking to get behind the boys, but needed some direction. Older, fatter and having drunk more than most of them, I would love to claim some fantastic witty response that got it all going, but it wasn't like that at all. A few 'Engerland' chants emerged in defiance before Monty, a veteran from the World Cup in '92, mentioned an inspirational song which got us going. 'We came here with our backpacks, you with ball and chains' and after a number of congas around the concrete paths that circled the GABBA and in front of the hill, that precipitated a hail of missiles and plastic cups, the Barmy Army was born.

We had got under the skin of the Aussies and, despite losing on the pitch, we had clearly found a winning formula in the stands as we taunted them over their weak dollar, the fact we owned their country and a personal favourite of mine to this day, *Captain Cook Only Stopped for a Shit!* Back then there were only about 30 of us who followed the whole tour, travelling on a budget, staying in hostels, purchasing cheap five day tickets with dodgy student passes procured in Thailand and living the dream.

Nobody really understood us then, the celebrated Sports Journalist Ian Wooldridge writing in the *Daily Mail* famously accused us of being the detritus of the British national social security system, morons who sought confrontation at every opportunity and he concluded that we should be gassed. For once he was way off the mark. Thankfully there has never been any trouble at any cricket ground anywhere in the world and we have built and developed a fantastic reputation for brilliant and loyal support and, most importantly, having great fun; win, lose or draw.

In the last 12 years thousands of fans have cottoned on to what we pioneered and made popular in the early 90's, largely due to to the fantastic coverage by Sky TV, who had beamed the fans having a fantastic time back into the UK's living rooms. Other factors contributed strongly. Recommendations and word of mouth from friends and family, cheap travel and a strong pound meant that suddenly watching England abroad became very popular.

Unlike the early years when England were getting soundly beaten away from home, in recent seasons we've been travelling with real confidence, and in November 2006 we arrived in Australia as holders of the Ashes and, with the Australians having an aging side, we had every reason to be believe that this tour would be different. On previous visits we'd experienced victory in Adelaide, Melbourne and Sydney, which sparked incredible scenes and wild celebrations and this time I really thought we could win two of the Tests to draw the series. The fact it all went pear-shaped on the pitch for Freddie and his men is an eminently forgettable footnote for *Wisden* and cricket history. For the thousands who made the trip it is all about the stories, the laughs and the personal memories and this book should now become a must read for anyone wanting to follow in our footsteps and watch the boys overseas while revelling in the experience.

One of my favourite Barmy Army quotes of all time goes to the *Sunday Sport* who stated that the Barmy Army outdrank, outsung and outshagged the Australians over the winter of 2006/7. My only regret is that in *Ashes To Dust* Graham Cookson concentrates too heavily on the first two points in his book! It is quite clear that the Aussie cricket fan has not evolved much in twelve years and I was in stitches reading about many of the incidents Graham recalls. They will ring true for every cricket fan who has followed England abroad, and for all those who harbour hopes of being able to do so in the future. We might have been losers on the pitch, but when it comes to humour, wit and atmosphere then we're the best in the business.

On a more serious note the book highlights the disgraceful way in which the England fans were ripped off, having to buy tickets at massive premiums just to watch the game. Couple that with the fact that Cricket Australia did their utmost to separate all of the Barmy Army-style supporters and then ejected our iconic trumpeter Billy from the first two Tests. These are three issues that must be addressed before the next tour. It proves, though, how important we have become to England, and how far we have got up Australian noses and into their consciousness.

On behalf of all the travelling fans, for the next Ashes series in 2010/11 the Barmy Army will demand that we do not pay more than the Fanatic sitting next to us, that we will not be split up in the grounds having travelled thousands of miles and spent thousands of pounds to watch the game and, finally, that Cricket Australia don't ban the one person who does more than anyone to set the positive tone and atmosphere for all of the crowd. To their credit the support we received from the Australian cricket public and media was unwavering and it made Billy Cooper one of the most talked about individuals in the whole series, attracting more and bigger headlines than some of the players.

This is the first time that anyone has ever taken the time to really tell the true story of what it is really like to follow a whole tour as a footsoldier with the Barmy Army. It is a fantastic insight and extremely funny, and I have great pleasure in recommending it to anyone who is looking to fulfil their own lifetime's ambition and watch the ultimate Test Series, the Ashes in Australia.

I hope to see you in the Lucky Shag in 2010/11.

Dave 'The General' Peacock
Founder & General, The Barmy Army

INTRODUCTION

Come with me if you will on a journey back to August 2005 and a golden summer.

This great country of ours was in the throes of a shocking and unexpected epidemic; cricket fever. The football season had started, but was widely being ignored as The Ashes took centre stage. Amazingly, in a pulsating and gut-wrenchingly exciting series, England beat the invincible Aussies. Get in.

Many women, and indeed some men, in workplaces and homes all around the nation asked obtuse questions about what was going on. This was a ritual usually reserved for World Cups and Henmania week two. We hadn't had a sniff of winning an Ashes Series for aeons, and suddenly, England had done it.

After the climax of the fifth Test, the Oval was drenched with emotion; then the players got absolutely leathered and trolleyed off to 10 Downing Street, open top bus rides and even a trip to Buck House ensued. What a superb achievement.

Andrew "Freddie" Flintoff was our talisman, the new Ian Botham only better. In fact it almost seemed as though Ian Botham was the old Freddie Flintoff, such was the burly Lancastrian's dominance in the series. Our Freddie could maybe even drink more than Beefy Botham (A contest which could be likened to football violence, fascinating to watch, but in no way would you want to get involved).

He was more Superman than Flintstone.

Under the strict laws of human sporting nature, it is perfectly normal to get greedy on such joyous occasions, and my thoughts were already turning to the following winter. I'm sure these musings were shared by many, many more. There could surely only be one thing better than turning over those cussed Australians on England's green and pleasant cricket grounds - sticking it right up 'em Down Under.

Let's face facts, the worm had turned. We'd finally out-Aussied the Aussies. We were more aggressive, more youthful, more imaginative and just plain better. Their creaking players, well past their sell-by date, were yesterday's men. It was a classic case of a changing of the guard. What made it even better was that as English summers mirror Australian winters and vice versa, we only had about 15 months to wait for the opportunity to ram this point home once again in their backyard.

Once The Ashes 2006-07 schedule was confirmed, my plan began to formulate. Nice and conservative really, a safety first approach, Geoff Boycott would have been proud. Its beauty was its simplicity - go to the first two Test Matches. Still home by Christmas and New Year, no more than three weeks away and god forbid in the unlikely event that we were 2-0 down after two tests (I knew that was never going to happen), we'd still hold the Ashes when I left HMP Australia.

But as time went on and the winter of 2005 turned into the spring of 2006, with the series just six months away, this strategy only scratched the itch a little bit. Having spent 13 years working at the same place, stagnation had really started to kick in. Basically, I'd been drifting longer than Tony Bullimore. Following the downbeat home Test Matches in 2006 from my workstation, it was clear that matches against Sri Lanka and Pakistan were a meagre popadom to the Beef Vindaloo with Pilau Rice and a Garlic Naan that was the Ashes series.

Then, as if by magic, it looked as though everything was starting to make sense. There was a strong possibility that my perfect scenario was about to unfold. The Holy Grail, the two magic words which so many office lifers crave more than any others; Voluntary Redundancy. This would have been my golden ticket, my Charlie Buckett moment. The timing would be spot on; four months paid notice followed by a nice wad of cash around November 2006. It's like it was meant to be.

How about going to all five Ashes Test Matches?

I'd developed a (wholly unpaid) hobby of doing a bit of writing; maybe this could be indulged at the same time. Something along the lines of 'Ashes Glory – giving the Aussies a proper shoe-ing on their own barren patch'. Brilliant. I could relay the joyous and victorious news to massed ranks in good old Blighty.

And this was my destiny calling because I had started my young life as an Aussie-phile.

The warm childhood memories of that strange but fascinating upside-down England were still vivid. First there was Rolf compelling us to 'Learn to Swim' (and who wouldn't trust a human beatbox who could paint as well) and then those Channel Nine highlights packages featuring a stranger and stranger looking Richie Benaud.

I had no idea he was an ex-cricketer. I just thought he was like a gentle human koala, brought in to present the sensitive side of Australia, in his pencil thin ties. He seemed affable, did Richie, possessing as he did the odd habit of looking sideways at the camera and saying 'Jen Embuwee' to identify one of our many 'not at the total peak of physical fitness' spinners. Always well turned out, a clean-shaven Aussie, which was quite something back then.

Aside from Monsieur Benaud, another facet of the childhood mystique was that this alien yet familiar country had great names for its cricket grounds. We had to endure bog standard stuff like The Oval (a shape) and Headingley (a suburb); they had the GABBA, the SCG and best of all for a cricket ground, the WACA. This one really captured my imagination.

When reporting from the WACA, the commentators on the radio kept going on about the Freemantle Doctor. Unsure what they meant, I created a picture of a combined old Father Time and WG Grace, but had no idea what the Doc was doing there. Maybe he was there to examine a girl who seemed to pre-occupy everybody's thoughts, Kerry Packer.

And it wasn't just the cricket. Our televisions became awash with Australian TV shows, *Neighbours, Home and Away, Young Doctors* and even the hugely confusing *Sons and Daughters*, I lapped it all up. I even stooped so low as to endure a depressing show called *The Sullivans*. The post-war lunchtime period drama cum soap was clearly a trap laid for anyone wanting to give school a swerve on some supposed illness. School was loads better than this.

Of course the Daddy of all the Aussie imports was appropriately enough *Prisoner Cell Block H*; a show which managed to be cheap, tacky, poorly acted with paper thin story lines and sets, but utterly compelling. Who could ever forget when Bea Smith was deposed as Top Dog and was demoted to a mere 'sheet folder' in the laundry? Go on, admit it, you loved it too. Right, OK, just me then.

So all things Australian seemed fascinating, but quickly my childish devotion turned to a teenage angst. I was, and still am, a pretty competitive kid and, like all my mates, sport was the most important thing in life. The stark reality was that we started to lose to Australia all the time. God, it's so unfair, I'm going to my room.

And, as if regular defeat was not enough, next came the pain of Waugh-gate. Not the barrier blocking access to Steve Harmison's parents' garden path, but an agonising episode involving me and the future Australia captain.

It was a beautiful day at Old Trafford (honest) for a one-day international in the early-1990s. I'd already had a gutful of England losing to the Aussies at most things, but especially cricket. Then it happened, the one incident to really harden my resolve.

Steve Waugh, already becoming England's nemesis, was fielding right in front of me on the boundary. A few lads behind me were constantly baiting him with: "where's your sheep, Waugh?" I was quite enjoying this. Not the wittiest jibe ever heard, but it was nice to hear someone 'sticking it to the Aussies.' After all, they were the 'sledging' world champions and any attempt to put them o ff their imperious stride would help our cause. Junior's older brother looked around tetchily and irritated, especially as, during one of his spells as a medium pace bowler, he'd just been smashed around in his previous over. Then I realised he thought I was the heckler. Gulp.

Waugh: Is that your first beer mate?
Me (quick as a flash): No mate, is this your first one-day international? Coz that over was shit.

I've had about 15 years to think of that.
What I really mumbled was: "Er, nah."
Like so many Englishmen before and since, I'd been psyched out on the verbals by these tough Aussies. I felt like a boy trying to cut it in a man's world. One day, not sure when, I would get my own back. Humiliated, I sat quietly as they subjected England to another inevitable defeat.

This was around the start of the Mark Taylor era and England just got battered every time we turned up for the Ashes. The pattern was well established; the Aussies race into a decisive lead, then ease up, go on the beer and maybe let us win a dead rubber at the end of the series.

In 1998 I took my first trip Down Under for the cricket, but it was more in hope than expectation supporting a distinctly average England side. By then, Taylor's reign was coming to an end and my sworn enemy Steven Roger Waugh was on the brink of becoming the captain.

This sojourn was relatively successful, witnessing an England Test win at the MCG, before they went on to Sydney and lost. The MCG Test was memorable in the sense that it contained the longest day in Test Match cricket history - eight hours and two minutes. Despite this significant event, Australia had already retained the Ashes before I even set foot in Manchester (does anybody still call it Ringway?) Airport.

It was also a chance to experience what I already suspected all along, the Aussie supporters are very bullish when they're winning. Another nugget of information that was probably obvious to everybody else, those Australians really love their sport, which makes beating them all the more pleasurable. Despite thoroughly enjoying the visit, it also served to add fuel to my now rampant anti-antipodean fire. The view was firmly entrenched now; whatever the sport, if an Aussie was involved, I supported the other side.

Fast forward to my next encounter, that glorious summer of 2005. I even went some way towards expunging the demons of Waugh-gate. Day Two of the Old Trafford Test saw me and my co-drinkers unceremoniously plonked in front of a group of Aussie lads. Although the Australian patter started brightly, as the lager flowed these lads got mercilessly picked apart by the now successful and alcohol-fuelled England support. They tried their best to match us jibe for jibe, but once it had been established that the Australian contribution to world comedy was Dame Edna, Joe Mangel and

Crocodile Dundee, just like their team, they were losing a fighting battle.

Showing true Aussie grit, they turned their attention back to the cricket and gave the much-maligned Ashley Giles a proper maligning. What they, us, Ashley and both teams didn't expect was that this was the day The King of Spain got it spot on. Oh how we laughed, as he cleaned up the much vaunted Australian top order to put England firmly in control. Despite the fact that England didn't ultimately win that match - rain and a brilliant Ricky Ponting innings saved the Aussies - we were the better side and eventually got our just deserts at The Oval.

Many cricket experts failed to predict that particular series victory, believing the 2005 series would come just a tad too early and expecting England's band of youngsters to rise up in the subsequent Ashes Tour. Australia 2006/7 was going to be the true turning point. This was when our golden crop of players would be at the peak of their powers, and the ancient Aussies would either quit or be washed up anyway.

So, as you can imagine, the start of England's period of dominance was going to be a sight to behold and something I just had to see.

When you think everything is going to plan, life has a habit of bringing you back into line a little bit. My golden ticket had been snatched away, some other kid had got that Wonka bar, there was to be no Voluntary Redundancy for me. Still, to unnecessarily stretch the chocolate analogy, as the great Paul Calf said: "In every sack of shite there's a spark of gold. You don't know, it might be an old Caramac wrapper, but it's there." For once in my life I knew what I wanted to do, even if I couldn't really afford it.

What followed was a period of despondency. My long-range forecast had been two months of bright sunshine in Australia. Now the prognosis was sitting under a dark cloud in a job I really didn't want. I was even boring myself with moaning about my situation, so I decided to do something impulsive and handed in my notice.

The hardest part was plucking up the courage to tell my parents. Strange but true for a 30-something. After that I was well on my way. It had to be done, I wasn't missing this. End of story. We had the Ashes in our hands. We only needed to draw the series in Australia to retain them, so even easier really. What's more, Freddie was now our captain, leading our brave lads into battle.

So after waiting seemingly ages, it was with huge excitement I headed off to Brisbane. Not just looking forward to the cricket, but revelling in the prospect of rubbing those cocky Aussies' noses right in it.

QUEENSLAND:
THE SUNSHINE STATE

"ALL AUSTRALIANS ARE AN UNEDUCATED AND
UNRULY MOB."

DOUGLAS JARDINE
(ENGLAND CRICKET CAPTAIN, 1932)

21 November - Arrive Brisbane

Having endured and enjoyed a flight packed with expectant English cricket fans, we finally made it to Brisbane.

Now the start of the Ashes series was getting closer, it seemed that rubbing the Aussies' noses in it was going to be a little bit tougher than first thought. To start with, getting hold of tickets had been a total nightmare.

My best approach would probably have been to get hold of as many tickets as possible pre-trip and then take a chance with the missing ones through touts and England fans with spares. But when you are a worrier and you've set out your stall to go to every day of every Test, asserting this to anyone who'll listen, it starts to eat away at you. So I eventually spent hours poring over ebay and a few sleepless nights phoning Australia. This experience was made worse by the fact that the Australian ticket agencies share the country's lack of musical taste, so the hold music tends to be excruciating.

Ultimately by hook (using Aussie contacts) and by crook (e-bay), plus using the Barmy Army and the commendable 'stoptout' website, I got the lot. This cost the thick end of around 800 quid, probably around four times the face value. Never mind, it'll be well worth it.

This problem stems from the Aussies taking the wholly unexpected loss of The Ashes quite badly and doing everything in their powers to make it difficult for the England fans. The austere organisation that is Cricket Australia came up with a scam that offered initial tickets sales to Australian residents only. They also got first refusal on ten tickets per day. This seems hugely excessive for an enormously popular event, especially as there are some Australian towns that don't even have a population of ten.

But this is a calculated ploy. The general feeling was that the Australians were put off their stride by the ferocity of England players and their fans last summer. It's certainly true of Jason Gillespie, who seemed totally unnerved by polite enquiries about the exact location of his mobile homestead.

As Ricky Ponting himself said when the ticket announcements were made.

""The Australian team can't wait for this Ashes series to start and having a sea of green and gold supporters in the stand will give us a massive boost".

Two things really, Ricky. First, let's face it, it's yellow not gold. Do Norwich play in gold? Nope, they play in canary yellow. Next, judging from the number of visitors around Brisbane right now, there will be plenty of English flotsam and jetsam floating around in that sea of yours.

What Ricky might have said is: "The Australian team can't wait for this Ashes series to start and we would like to give a sea of scalpers from both Australia and the UK a massive boost." Incidentally, a scalper is the Australian's far superior name for what the British would know as a ticket tout.

All this stuff will just make our forthcoming victory all the sweeter.

There also seems to have been a concerted effort to spread scare stories about how the England fans might behave. This is just mischievous and seems to be based on an old fashioned view of the football hooligan. Most rational people realise that although many of the English wear football shirts, fighting at the cricket just isn't the done thing. And seriously, does anyone who wears a football shirt actually cause any bother anyway? If it was the Stone Island army coming over you could maybe understand it.

To combat this imaginary threat comes the 'Dob in a Yob' scheme. All you need to do is text the seat number of a trouble-maker near you and the authorities will arrive promptly to dissipate the situation. Whether this translates to 'Shop a Pom' remains to be seen. Maybe the best text cricketer of all time, Shane Warne, will benefit from this service.

So hard going for the fans and things haven't exactly been going to plan for the England team either. Already robbed of Simon Jones, Michael Vaughan and Marcus Trescothick, dubbed Stresscothick over here, England suffered the trademark opening fixture defeat against the Prime Minister's XI.

There have also been some rumblings around team selection. The perceived wisdom, supported by their performances in the summer series against Pakistan, was that both Chris Read and Monty Panesar were certain starters. It's already been announced that Geraint Jones will start as wicket-keeper but the word from the media people in the know, is that the spinner's place will go to Ashes stalwart Ashley Giles. In a Chris Kirkland-type way, Ashley seems to have enhanced his prospects by not playing at all.

As sport fans, we've all had those moments when you think the coach/manager has made a major error. There are also those coaches who have done so much to improve your team that you just have to give them the benefit of the doubt. Duncan Fletcher knows what's required. After all, he was our first Ashes winning coach for 18 years and he knows what it will take to retain them.

However in George Orwell's *1984* Winston Smith was described as a lunatic, because he preferred to be a minority of one. Well it maybe isn't that bad but there seem to be very few who support the dour Zimbabwean's point of view, especially about Giles. But Duncan Fletcher has transformed English cricket. So it has to be a case of 'In Duncan we trust, let the good times roll'. Maybe Gilo will have one of those days like Old Trafford last year.

Maybe it's the lager we've had to negate the potential of jet lag but me and my travelling companion, Matt, remain optimistic. In fact, Matt has been completely positive in his outlook, happily reminding me that if it hadn't been for the rain in the last series we'd have won 4-1. He's expecting a convincing England series win. Is this rosy outlook associated with being a Bradford City fan? Who knows?

We've decided that Trescothick was struggling anyway so his absence just takes away a selection headache. In fact, we were feeling so upbeat that we put a bet on Shane Warne not to get his 700th wicket in the series.

Only two more sleeps until the First Test. Eek.

22 November - Brisbane

Brisbane is a nice looking place, no mistake. The shiny Central Business District is really modern and the city is interspersed with the imaginatively named Brisbane River. Let us not forget that this country also boasts the Great Sandy Desert and the Snowy Mountains. Anyway, riverside drinking and dining are a rare pleasure and naturally the Sunshine State has the climate.

Funny old bunch so far the Queenslanders. Many claim to be staunchly Republican despite the fact that in a cruel twist most of their main streets are named after, to quote them, 'blahddy pommie monarchs'.

It's always fascinating to visit another country and try to establish (and maybe even play on) the regional differences. We sweepingly generalise Aussies as a certain breed but in a country 60 times bigger than England there are bound to be nuances. I'd already got the impression that Sydney and Melbourne residents had a superiority complex over each other and the rest of Australia, but it was my first time in a rival state capital.

Dining in a city centre restaurant, it was a bit of a shock to hear the views of our resident restauranteur. Sophisticated sort he was, well spoken, very smartly dressed. To put it in the most polite cricketing terms, he probably took his bowling from the pavilion end but this has no bearing on anything, just trying to paint the picture. When quizzed about the rivalry/difference between Brisbane and the other cities he was quite brutal.

"If I was to go to Sydney or Melbourne and say I was from Queensland, they'd assume I was retarded." And he was deadly serious.

This was a bit of a shocker as we had seen no supporting evidence of this whatsoever, the people of Queensland had been unerringly polite and seemed genuinely pleased to welcome visitors who had made such a long journey for something as trivial as cricket. Brisbane was a really smart and laid-back place, and the hosts had really been so far so good.

Welcome wise, the England cricket team hadn't enjoyed Australia too much as both Monty Panesar and Kevin Pietersen had been subjected to racial abuse. Now whatever your own personal view of political correctness, one thing is for sure, Australia is nowhere near as far down the road as we are in the UK. If you look at it in M62 terms, the UK is over halfway there, just up near Warrington, around IKEA, the Aussies have broken down just outside Hull.

The slur facing Monty was that he's an 'Indian Idiot'. Again, not the most offensive words ever uttered but as well as having bad intentions, it was wrong on both counts. You see, university graduate Monty was born in Bedfordshire, Luton to be precise old chap.

As far as the cricket goes, England have struggled in the warm-up games but gradually improved, supporting the view that they are peaking at exactly the right time. The management regime has seemed pretty relaxed about the whole series for a long time now. Reaction to such issues as the defection of bowling guru Troy Cooley to the Australian camp seemed somewhat blasé. The Aussie Cooley was perceived to have had a profound effect on the England bowlers and ultimately to the outcome of the 2005 series.

The appointment of Flintoff as captain also seems like a risky one. England have made the mistake in the past of saddling their best player with the responsibility, most notably when Freddie Mark One himself, Ian Botham, had an absolute nightmare with the bat when made captain.

There are two possible explanations

1. England are supremely confident about the forthcoming series
2. England have been very complacent since the Ashes win

Call it men's intuition if you like but I've got the distinct impression it's the first one.

There was a surprise for all England fans today, there were still tickets for Day One on sale. After all the talk of sell-outs, and

Cricket Australia definitely sold-out, it was possible to get a ticket the day before the Test.

Despite this the anticipation is really building. Nobody could claim the British Media, especially the Press, are paragons of fair play and virtue, but the Australian media take it to the next level. The papers have been crammed full of journos and ex-players announcing the inevitability of an Aussie win in the First Test, and Rupert Murdoch's Fox Channel are just amazing. Their coverage, before the Test has even started, makes a Cyclops look very two-eyed. To stoke it up further, they showed a classic Channel Nine match between Australia and England staged at the GABBA from the 82/83 tour. It was classic in the sense that Australia murdered us and cruised home by 7 wickets, we had two awful run-outs and somebody released a pig onto the outfield with the word Botham daubed on it in paint.

The other big news story is that Ian 'The Thorpedo' Thorpe has quit swimming at the tender age of 24, after consulting his mystery adviser. His actions have been described as 'Un-Australian' in some quarters and there are various rumours surrounding his 'lifestyle choices'. The news channels seem to have abandoned Iraq, Afghanistan and all that stuff now. All they can squeeze in between the sport is weather news.

And it's going to be pretty damn warm at the GABBA tomorrow. Come on England.

23 November – Day 1 Brisbane Test
Australia 346-3

So to the Woolongabba, or simply the GABBA as it is more commonly known, for Day One.

The name is Aboriginal, but there are two separate theories

about the derivation. It either means "whirling water", which seems pretty unlikely in arid Queensland, or "fight talk place", which is fighting talk where I come from. Looking back on the first day, I suspect it is the latter.

The GABBA is on the other side of town, and about a 45-minute walk or in this case a 20-minute journey on the sauna on wheels they call a bus. It was pretty much gridlock on the roads and even the bus lane was chocka, a sign of the eagerness to be there to see first ball.

The stadium itself is modern and impressive, totally purpose built. The problem is that the purpose is not cricket, but Aussie Rules Football, or 'fuddy' as the natives call it. What faced the England players and fans was a totally symmetrical stadium with a bear-pit of an atmosphere. Ask most people to describe the perfect cricket ground and they will probably wax lyrical about magnificent trees, green grass banks, quaint pavilions and traditional scoreboards, operated by man not machine.

The GABBA had none of these. Truly a bowl with no soul. It is usually scheduled for the First Test of the Ashes tour but if Cricket Australia wanted to choose a less welcoming venue, they'd struggle. Perfect for what they had in mind, smashing England to pieces even smaller than smithereens.

Giles and Jones were playing, a decision greeted with bemusement by Australians and English alike, and England had experienced the misfortune of losing the toss. So we'd see the Australians bat first.

Day One was a pretty hot day and we were deposited in the glaring sun for the start of play. Luckily I was already doused in Factor 30+ having been accosted in the chemist the day before as I idly browsed through the Factor 15. "If you're going to the cricket, you need Factor 30 plus" I was emphatically informed. She was so right. I was a bit paranoid about getting fried anyway. My last trip had culminated with a day on Manly Beach, trying to get 'a proper sun tan'. 24 hours in economy with blistered skin doesn't really help the trip home.

The quest to retain The Ashes seemed to have had a pretty profound effect on the locals, who were at fever pitch by the time the players took the field. A baying wall of largely incomprehensible noise. There were a few less English people around me than I'd anticipated; this wasn't going to be a home-from-home match. It was Steve Harmison to bowl the first ball. Grievous Bodily Harmison, the man who had done so much to set the tone the previous summer by making the Aussies jump around with his searing pace and bounce.

My only thought, and I'm sure the overwhelming thought of the England fans at the game was, "Come on Harmy, shut these fuckers up."

So as David Coleman used to say when *Question of Sport* really mattered, "what happened next?"

WIDE

There was a momentary pause, a collective gasp and then the Aussies went completely mental. As in all sports there is sometimes a greater sense of joy in seeing an opponent dropping a clanger than seeing your favourite player do something amazing. Many Australians probably couldn't spell Schadenfreude, but they could have invented it.

"Put him on at both ends"

"Harmison, I've got your mum on the phone"

And so on and so on. In fairness, the notoriously home-sick Harmy looked like he'd gladly take the next plane home. It wasn't until seeing the TV replays that I'd realised just how wide that first ball was, being taken at second slip. It was akin to having a penalty at football and hitting the corner flag.

Several commentators stated at close of play that this ball

might have set the tone for the whole series. What, one delivery out of about 13,000? Behave. It was pretty representative of the early exchanges though, with England bowlers just too inaccurate and Australia racing to 57-0 after the first hour of play. It was also clear in this period that the Australian players, fans and administrators were not about to make the visitors especially welcome.

Ford had launched a 'Tonk a Pom' campaign and every time the ball raced to the boundary, whether off the middle of the bat or the edge, the word 'Tonked' was emblazoned on the big screen. As for the fans, well the signs were not great when a bloke with possibly the worst case of brickie's arse I have ever seen, positioned himself directly in the seat in front. To compliment the cleavage he also had a lifeguard swimming cap on. As he was such a big lad he would probably have been more use as one of those massive inflatables for a pool party as opposed to some kind of Ironman.

The problem for most people in our row, English and Australians alike, was that like a car accident or when you have stitches put in, you just can't help looking. Every time he went to stand up, which was a lot, this sight dominated the horizon. It goes without saying that our resident lifesaver was loud and boorish, whooping and hollering at every available opportunity. As the Aussies took control in the afternoon session, he decided to treat us to that classic ditty, *I'd Rather Be A Poofter Than A Pom*. It was at this stage I felt the need offer a stolid defence.

Me: What's wrong with being both mate. To be honest, we're only really looking forward to the Sydney Test so we can go to the Mardi Gras.

Lifebuoy: Silence

In fact that scuppered him for almost 20 minutes, which was a result of sorts.

Queensland: The Sunshine State

This was a rare oasis of calm on a boisterous day. Mark Twain once said "it is better to keep your mouth shut and appear stupid than to open it and remove all doubt."

The Australians in the GABBA appeared to live by the exact opposite of this tenet. Another example was the wag who called Jimmy Anderson a midget throughout and offered him a stepladder to get over the rope. Jimmy's probably about 6'2" so I felt the need to point this out to the vocal one. I asked him to stand up because I couldn't hear him properly, of course he already was.

The final indignation, on a day when the relatively small number of England fans in our section really held their own, took place later in the day. It was still like an oven in the GABBA and the Aussies were cruising by now. England desperately needed a wicket to break the ominous Ponting/Hussey partnership. Kiwi umpire and general showman Billy Bowden appeared to raise his finger in response to a sustained appeal. A crumb of comfort on an otherwise difficult day I was on my feet, waving the Union Jack around and generally doing my nut. But it turned out that Billy's extravagant gesture was a mere scratch of the nose.

And didn't the locals just love pointing out that fact. Yeah, cheers Billy. So a tough day at the GABBA for all concerned, and you already suspected that England would kill for a draw in the First Test.

November 24 – Day 2 Brisbane Test
Australia 602-9 declared
England 53-3

Maybe now we'd kill to take it into a fourth day. You need to know very little about cricket to know from those scores that England had taken a pummelling over the first two days, and how.

The day started badly with a seat even further forward in the bear-pit, about three rows from the front to be precise. This guaranteed all day sunshine with about five minutes of respite when it cheekily hid behind one of the GABBA's huge floodlight pylons. So a seat in the heat was a set-back, being sat close to some more Aussie muppets was another kick in bails really.

There are a couple of points to make clear at this stage. Not every Aussie in the crowd was an idiot; in fact, several were genuinely ashamed of the behaviour of the most irritating element. Apparently, one of the reasons why the 'Mexican Wave' is frowned upon in Australian cricket grounds is that some patrons of the GABBA take the opportunity to relieve themselves in their empty plastic beer glasses and lob the contents into the air when the wave gets around. Mmmm, nice. But, in fairness, a lot of them were pretty sound, it just seems like a Darwinian own goal that they turned out to be the quieter ones.

Point two is that I am no way a fighter. It's important to speak up for your team, friends or whatever, but if there had been any bother I would have been off in the opposite direction pronto. Verbal sparring is good fun however.

After a few minutes, some bright spark piped up with a twist on yesterday's classic ditty, this time 'I'd rather be a paki than a pom'. There had been a lot of brouhaha before the series about racism so I thought I'd point out to this youngster that he couldn't sing that because it was racist. And that it would be shame for him to get thrown out.

The reaction of incredulity was a bit of a shock as the perpetrator and all his mates were amazed that this could be described as racist. Like I said, not too far down that PC road. These lads then further dignified themselves with a 30-minute diatribe to the England fielder on the boundary. "Bell, you're shit," "Bell, you midget" and "Look at the scoreboard, Bell. You're getting tonked,"etc etc. There was a wry smile on Paul Collingwood's face as he eventually jogged over to a different run saving position.

As for events on the pitch, England were run ragged in the field as the Australians built a formidable total. The biggest single reason for England's success last summer was their ability to restrict Australia to scores of less than 400 on every single occasion. They passed that benchmark with ease and it was extremely worrying.

We also got a little insight into what it was like to be a professional cricketer playing on the unforgiving cricket fields of Australia. Alastair Cook, in his First Test against the Aussies, was presented with a skyer that seemed to be in the air for ages. He was staring into the blinding sunshine and the locals sensed blood. The rising cacophony of noise was almost unbearable as you willed him to catch it. He looked a bit shaky but you could picture him pouching it and giving a little wave to the baying hoards. In the end, he didn't really get that close to the ball. Even more so than the previous day when Harmison had pinged down a wide, the noise was deafening. No fun for us, even less so for one A.N. Cook.

After the indignity of Australia racking up 600 and even their Number 10 Stuart Clark (who?) scoring 39 in 23 balls, it was Alastair's big chance to fulfil his primary function on the tour, making big runs at the top of the order. This was always going to be a tricky last hour with all the momentum, unlike The Ashes, in Australia's hands.

Having seen his opening partner get out to an injudicious shot to Glenn McGrath, Cook faced the 'surely past it by now' paceman's next ball. Edged, OUT. Straight to, who else but the Daddy of the Dad's Army, Shane Warne. The noise just got bigger. My newly formed sworn enemies in front thought this would be a good time for a rendition of *I'd Rather Be A Poofter Than A Pom*. Yesterday's Mardi Gras approach seemed as good as any so I trotted that one out again. Then their biggest mouth took over;

Mouth: Shut up dickhead. Look at the fucking scoreboard man, you're getting flogged.

Me: Mate I'm flattered, but you're just not my type.

It stopped him in his tracks for a minute or two anyway.

The England players weren't really helping themselves and by close of play England had lost yet another wicket and would need a miracle to avoid the follow on, let alone force a draw. Perhaps this trip wasn't such a brilliant idea after all. But wait, enough of that defeatist talk, even if, and it is still an if, we lose this one, didn't we lose the First Test in 2005?

More evidence of the fact that the Aussies were playing hardball had befallen the Barmy Army. The recent Tourism Australia ad campaign bore the slogan 'Australia, so where the bloody hell are you?'. Well in the case of Billy Cooper, the Barmy Army trumpeter, he wasn't in the GABBA. He'd been kicked out on Day One. His heinous crime? Hitting someone with his trumpet? Nope, try again. It was playing the *Neighbours* theme.

That's when good neighbours become good friends.

November 25 – Day 3 Brisbane Test
Australia 602-9 dec and 181-1
England 157

As today's random seat was based in the upper tier of the GABBA, our neighbours were a major contrast to those of the first two days. This area housed a relatively refined clientele and if anything was a bit too quiet and grown up. It did have one huge advantage though; it was in the shade.

Again it was pretty much a sell out and to give the Australian cricket authorities some credit (ouch, that hurt), they do make cricket accessible for the locals. The cost of a daily ticket was around 10 quid, about the same amount as you would pay to get into a county cricket match in England. For a Test back home, you could easily expect to pay three or four times this amount for the cheap seats.

So things were better off the pitch, but on it the carnage continued. That uber-Aussie himself Glenn McGrath had somehow mustered up a performance from his ageing limbs and taken six wickets. I couldn't stand McGrath, he was the archetypal cocky Australian. He regularly predicted 5-0 wins in the Ashes series (even the last one eh Glennda?), and had recently developed an even more irritating habit.

This was to name his 'bunnies' before the series started. It seems that he felt that a way of unsettling some of the opposition was to nominate in advance some players that he would regularly get out during the series. Surely this smacked of desperation from an old man who had shown in England that he was way past his best. Well apparently not. Oh yeah and his first two wickets, Strauss and Cook, his nominated bunnies.

McGrath is also the man I associate with the relatively new but unnecessary habit of holding the ball aloft when a bowler has taken five wickets. This seemed to be his one-man crusade to get equal rights for bowlers and batsmen. I hadn't really envisaged seeing him doing this in the First Test.

Just to make things worse, Flintoff was out for a duck and looked like he got a pretty dodgy decision. This gave the Aussies another chance to continue the psychological bombardment. There are two big screens in the GABBA, one acting as a scoreboard, the other showing replays. Curiously, both screens showed a replay of Freddie's wicket, the only replay on both screens that anyone could recall during the first three days. They had really put some thought into this.

Another strange phenomenon is the Aussie crowd's love of throwing inflatable stuff around the fans, mostly beachballs. There are serious cheers, oohs and aahs until the item meets it untimely death, confiscation by the officials. Day Three saw this idea taken further; a female blow up doll was tossed roughly around the crowd. At first it looked like a real woman, with the locals perhaps living down to the old reputation 'Australian women like to be treated badly and Australian men are only too happy to oblige'. But no, this one was inflatable.

It seemed like an appropriate time to resurrect an old joke so I leaned forward and said to the Aussie sat in front of me

"I used to have a blow up doll but it got a puncture - it kept going down on me."

My expectation was that he'd tell me what a lame joke it was or maybe get a little laugh, but no. My newfound friend proceeded to tell me about the most reliable makes of blow up doll and recommended a particular type guaranteed not to puncture. I promise you there was not even a hint of irony.

This puzzled me a bit but the main confusion around the rest of the GABBA was Ricky Ponting's decision not to enforce the follow on. Many of the locals thought this was a poor decision (they may have even considered it un-Australian) and felt that neither of Ricky's predecessors, Taylor or Waugh, would have made such a choice. My own view was that he was just trying to rub our noses in it and make England suffer as much as possible, but it still seemed a bit strange. Cricket seems to be about momentum and England were truly on their collective arses at that time.

In the end it probably doesn't matter, as it would take a miracle for England to avoid defeat. The promise of early showers on Day Five seems pretty irrelevant really. In Manchester if it rains for an hour you'll be deprived of play for a day, in Brisbane it's probably the exact opposite.

Queensland: The Sunshine State

Slightly bored by the match situation, and the lack of banter in the surroundings, we decided to head downstairs to Bay 25, where both sets of fans had started to gather and have a bit of a sing-off on a daily basis. You could tell that the Australians found the vocal support for the England team really bemusing, why would you want to support a team that was getting so badly beaten?

Several lemming-like Australians followed the same pattern.

1. Come over and try to shout the English lads down
2. When this failed start jostling people around
3. Get warned by the Police to calm down
4. Get even angrier and up the jostling
5. Get thrown out with a chorus of "Cheerio, Cheerio, Cheerio," ringing in their ears.

This happened loads of times and it really was a case of Multi Cheerios on Day Three.

It's strange that the Aussie fans really seem to take exception to being spoken to by the police. Anyone who regularly attends football matches will know that your chances of being spoken to at some point are pretty high, and that resistance is pretty much futile. The Aussies seem to take such umbrage that sure as night follows day they get the hard word and are gone five minutes later.

Now starting a chant at a sporting event is a fickle business. If everybody joins in, you can pat yourself on the back and shout "I started that," to anyone who will listen, above the rousing chorus of "your song". But it normally takes a special kind of person to handle the rejection, when it just doesn't take off for whatever reason.

Serial chant-starters are no doubt blatant womanisers or amazing sales-people, mainly because they can handle the knock-backs. So because I find rejection hard to handle, chant starting just isn't my thing. But when you see something so obvious, you've just got to get involved.

It suddenly occurred to me that one of the Aussie coppers had a really impressive beard and looked just like Chuck Norris. I'm a major fan of Chuck, not for his martial arts films, which I imagine are rubbish but will probably never find out, but for the websites which tell you top spoof facts about Mr Norris, as a testament to his hardness. Examples include: Chuck Norris has counted to infinity – twice, Chuck Norris can slam revolving doors and, my own personal favourite, Chuck Norris once took a bottle of sleeping pills and blinked once.

So imagine my pride when I managed to get a chant of "There's only one Chuck Norris" going, directed at the Aussie policeman, who responded with a rueful smile. If you don't believe me you can see Chuck (who looks as though he's picked out some-one in the distance to kill) on the front cover.

Due in no part to my measly contribution, it was no surprise that the sing-a-thon was easily won by the much more creative and tuneful England fans, with abundant references to the Queen guaranteed to raise the hackles of the Aussies. In fairness to them, they did come up with one partially coherent ditty, cruel though it was:

Que Sera, Sera
Whatever will be, will be
Trescothick's in therapy,
Que Sera Sera.

Not bad, very good for them.

The cricket meandered along as Australia established a ridiculously strong position. The most galling part was the fact that England's bowling looked totally innocuous. You just knew that as soon as the Australian bowlers got hold of the ball it would be a different story.

On the way back to our digs, Matt and I bumped into to Sky Sports' own David 'Bumble' Lloyd. We were still clutching at the straw that Ponting had made a mistake to bat on. Bumble was having none of it,

"Forget here lads, let's get to Adelaide."

He was probably right, but it would be nice to at least see England make a better fist of batting the second time around.

November 26 – Day 4 Brisbane Test
Australia 602-9 dec and 202-1 dec
England 157 and 293-5

And make a better fist of it they did.

I woke up in a slightly grouchy mood having witnessed a lacklustre Everton display against Charlton. It was a turgid 1-1 draw and hard going just to stay awake to be honest. The decision to forego my Goodison season ticket for four games, which had left me racked with guilt, was looking like a decent one if this performance was anything to go by.

However, there was some brighter news on the cricket front, we had somehow arrived at the ground early and took the opportunity to have a look at the England players in the nets. This also meant getting a long overdue look at Monty Panesar bowling.

And who was that lean, tall batsmen he was twirling them down to? None other than Mr Michael Vaughan. He seemed to be moving freely and just maybe there is a chance he'll figure in this series sooner rather than later. Based on England's feeble display both in the field and with the bat, a less than 100% Vaughan would be worth serious consideration.

The cavalcade of celebrity continued and as an ex-smoker myself, it is sometimes pleasant just to get a bit of passive smoking in. There is no better way of doing it than grabbing a photo opportunity with Phil Tufnell. I got a proper nose full. It was nice to see Tuffers, just when you think the heavy drinking and eating schedule is taking its toll, a few moments with the dishevelled *I'm A Celebrity* champ and you quickly realise that you're not looking too bad after all.

Clad in my Union Jack on the way around the ground, I also managed to get heckled by some of the many Kath and Kim types. It's amazing really, until this encounter I had assumed that the characters in that particular show are exaggerated, you know, in a kind of 'over the top Steve Irwin Aussie' type way. Little did I know that the programme is actually a pale imitation of the crassness of some of the Australian ladies.

Once in the ground, back in the sunshine but in a slightly saner area, it was a further surprise to see Australia batting on some more. They finally took the decision to declare once Justin Langer had reached his hundred, and it was a case of the end of the phoney war and the start of real hostilities once again.

And while the match had almost certainly gone, it was really pleasing to see England making a far better job of their second innings. Indeed they appeared to show more grit, determination and application than they had in the previous three days. This was heartening for those stranded in Australia for the next few weeks and augured well for the rest of the series.

It was a real shame to see Paul Collingwood getting out on 96, just short of a first Test century against the Aussies. He was out-foxed by Warne, who added four more wickets towards scuppering our bet. Damn. It was great to see Colly doing well, as many people will have questioned his right to be in the side, but he's a feisty sort and a brilliant fielder. Having lost a few of the experienced players before the series, England are going to need a lot of aggression to survive out here and Collingwood certainly has that.

Despite the match situation things are definitely looking up, with a few chinks in the so far imperious Aussie armour appearing. First, Ricky Ponting had to leave the field with a sore back and the latest news is that Glenn McGrath is troubled by a blister on his heel. Sorry Glenn, but you want to try walking for 45 minutes to the GABBA in a pair of sandals every day, then you'd know all about blisters.

Once again I took the opportunity to leave the relative tranquillity of my seat to go and join the sing-off in the rowdier section of the ground. The police and stewards seemed to be attempting to make amends for their earlier heavy-handedness with a charm offensive. They were spending most of their time taking pics of groups of England fans on demand. Just maybe somebody has reminded them what a lucrative cash cow their English visitors really are. In fairness to them, when you have a chat it sounds as though they are as unhappy with their orders to act as a 'fun police' as anybody else is. But there you go.

As far as the sing-song went, the Aussie fans let themselves down by using the term 'Paki' once again. Maybe this just isn't deemed as offensive over here, but it was still a shock to my ears to hear it sung so brazenly. It is starting to get easier to understand how former Aussie players such as Dean Jones and Darren Lehman have got themselves into trouble with racist comments in the past. And didn't Mel Gibson get up to something like that? A pattern emerging there maybe?

Having had their fill of *God Save YOUR Queen* and *You All Live In A Convict Colony* from us, the Aussie fans came up with *Warnie's Shagged Your Sister* in retaliation. I thought it was a chance to have a bit of fun with one Aussie so asked him,

Me: Sorry mate, what was that song, Warnie's shagged his sister?

Him: No mate, YOUR sister, that's why it's so funny

Never mind, forget it.

The seemingly endless conveyer belt of Aussie lemmings continued unabated and the fun police persisted in picking them off. There's only one thing that seems to upset the police about the England fans and that's the conga. No idea why.

After close of play we were just sitting down to eat something and there's a magical moment, a bit like snow on Christmas morning. It's raining, a bit. Halfway through Day Three and the game seemed hours from being over and now we've got some rain with a day to go. In a perverse and probably thoroughly English sense, it would be more satisfying to watch a day of rain than it would to see England bat the day out. Could this be shades of Egbaston 2005, when Ricky Ponting took the bizarre decision to put England in to bat, thus surrendering the advantage in the series, which his team never managed to regain? Maybe, just maybe, he's made an error of even more monstrous proportions.

On the assumption that there isn't a game-ending deluge, we probably have one hope tomorrow and that is Kevin Pietersen's presence at the crease. He's not everyone's cup of tea and based on some of the media reports you can understand why, but he is someone who displays tremendous self-belief. He will believe he can bat all day, maybe that would be better than a day of rain after all.

November 27 Day 5 – Brisbane Test
Australia 602-9 dec and 202-1 dec
England 157 and 370
Australia won by 277 runs

Queensland: The Sunshine State

Just for a moment it looked possible.

Brisbane's trademark 6am bright sunshine had been like someone shining a massive spotlight through the window every morning. This was absent today, failing for once to add body clock insult to cricket injury. The sky had a slightly grey feel to it so you thought just maybe the thirst of the England cricket fans and the Queensland farmers would be satiated at the same time.

In fact it turned out to be a quick kill for the Aussies as KP was out early and the increasingly fine weather put paid to any hope. So much for Queensland's first decent rain for about 20 years. In reality the game had been lost in the first three days, not this morning.

Surprisingly it was a case of 'spot the Aussie' in the ground, with England fans making up the vast majority of a sparse crowd. This gave the visitors a chance to congregate and the Barmy Army to be heard in full voice. The Barmy Army went through the impressive repertoire of songs, including a gentle reminder to Brett Lee to 'keep your arm straight when you bowl', which is merely there to do him a favour and is to be commended.

The Barmy Army have also developed a song based around the Newcastle United chant about being the 'loyalest supporters the world has ever had.' Hmmm, not too sure about this one. Apart from the blatant grammatical problems, I've always found it a little bit self-congratulatory, although the words are probably true of the England cricket fans, if not Newcastle's. There's also a touch of the Colin Hunt's about a self-professed claim of 'we are mental, and we are mad'.

But that's all splitting hairs really. The Barmies support of England on the final day is exemplary and when the Australians drive the final nail into the coffin, the England fans can still be heard supporting their team. At close of play, the England players came over to acknowledge the support and in fairness seemed to get the balance right between expressing their gratitude and looking a little sheepish about their performance. They must know that loads better is expected of them. We are all acutely aware that after such a comprehensive defeat it's going to be tough to get it back from here.

The fact is they did make a better go of it in the 2nd innings. 370 is a decent score second time around in just about any game, 157 is a paltry 1st innings score under all circumstances. England would stand a much better chance if they picked the right team and this would involve bringing in Read and Panesar for Giles and Jones. It may well be worth giving Mahmood a go ahead of that midget Anderson too.

In order to cleanse yourself of the GABBA experience, there's only one thing to do and that's to get really drunk. At least this is possible safe in the knowledge that there will be no early start to get to the cricket for 10am. I've had a few snorts of derision from home when I explained what a punishing schedule it is over here; a typical day has been something like this

1. Get up about 8am
2. Get showered
3. Breakfast
4. A few pissy mid-strength Aussie beers (coz that's all they trust the locals with) during the day
5. Get out on the booze with some food thrown in at some point
6. Stay up all night watching live English football
7. Repeat to fade

I'm sure you'll agree that this is seriously hard going.

Queensland: The Sunshine State

28 November – Brisbane

The going is even tougher today, my head really hurts. Tuesday's going to be a bit of a write-off. So a few random musings now the cricket's over for a little while.

It's always great to watch TV in another country and Australia is no exception. The Aussie media are having a field day today about how their boys have 'stuck it to the poms' and it quickly becomes apparent just how big a deal the Australian cricket team is in this country. Clearly they have been the World's Number 1 team for a long time now but the amount of coverage and exposure afforded to them is still astonishing.

The distinctly average Brett Lee advertises breakfast cereal and Mike Hussey, a relative newcomer to the team (I know, he's made a brilliant start) promotes Qantas. The biggest shock is to see Brad Hogg in an advert for MasterCard. Brad who?

For those who don't know, Brad is regular member of the Australian one-day side and is a World Cup winner. But looking at this in another way, he's the Australian equivalent of our own Jamie Dalrymple. And to coin someone else's phrase, originally in reference to Everton's Tobias Linderoth, Jamie could walk in here with a big luminous sign above his head saying I AM JAMIE DALRYMPLE, and you'd still feel duty bound to ask, "Who are you?"

It seems as though the only two sports enjoying national popularity in Australia are Cricket and Aussie Rules. As it is not possible to have a national team for Aussie Rules, as no one else plays the game where everyone appears to have forgotten their shirts, the Aussie cricketers are the national icons.

Another curiosity of Australian media life is one of the favourite phrases they just love to coin, 'he'd make a great Aussie.' In this particular case it was a reference to Kevin Pietersen, based on the fact that he shows confidence and self-belief and is really good at cricket. This seems reminiscent of the psychopath Begbie in Trainspotting. Despite being a total nutter he constructs imaginary qualities in his friends and then shamelessly awards them to himself. And nobody on TV can spew out the name Kevin Pietersen without the obligatory prefix of 'South African-born'.

Another somewhat casual observation about Australia and Aussie men is that absolutely loads of them are sporting moustaches. This country has been the home to some serious fashion faux pas over the years, including the ubiquitous blond highlights, but this is just strange. Proper big handlebar ones as well, horrible.

As you can probably sense, today has been a bit of a non-event. The highlight was probably the realisation that our hotel was served by a company called Schindler's Lifts, good that.

Two more days' respite and then it's the Second Test, they don't half come around quick. We're going to the zoo tomorrow, we can stay all day.

November 29 - Brisbane

The point was that we really couldn't stay all day and shouldn't have gone to the zoo at all, but more of that later.

Steve Irwin was in a select band of people, a genuinely likeable Australian. I'd developed an affection for the khaki-clad one when lodging at a mate's house. We used to get a bit wasted and then laugh our heads off at Steve and his antics. My own personal favourite was when he gently cajoled a shark, cruelly caught in a fishing net, to freedom. He dubbed his voiceovers on later but for him to say "Now Oim caught in the net!" was priceless as he struggled to free himself. The shark was long gone. Brilliant.

My devotion to Steve was such that I had already named my Fantasy Ashes team in his honour and had even taken my niece to see his movie. This was an unpleasant Hollywood bastardisation of his work, but his ham acting was still really quite funny. So the chance to visit Australia Zoo, Irwin's very own, was too good to miss. And all it took to get there was an hour on the train and a quick coach ride. Just round the corner in vast Aussie terms.

The exhibits were pretty impressive, but it was disappointing to note that Harriet, the 176-year-old giant tortoise, had also met a sad demise in 2006. Rumours that she was on the brink of a call up to the ageing Australian cricket squad remained unconfirmed at the time of her passing.

Zoos are pretty similar the world over but the most memorable aspect of this one was all the tributes to Steve Irwin. Loads and loads of his trademark khaki shirts, festooned with heartfelt written tributes to him. There were also a copious number of accolades from school kids; you could almost imagine them pestering their teachers to allow them to do what they wanted to, pay homage to a real TV star. It's very easy (and sometimes quite good fun) to be cynical about this sort of thing, the Princess Di reaction seemed way over the top to me, but this was really touching stuff.

And his legacy lives on just fine. Having watched the crocodile show there are plenty of successors who are seemingly willing to tease crocodiles to the brink of attack, just being able to withdraw in a timely manner. Hearing the croc smash its jaws together to devour some raw meat was both inspiring and frightening at the same time.

Bit like the Aussie Team at the GABBA.

Away from the cricket, and the ubiquitous bush fires, the big media story today surrounds The Wiggles. Greg Page, the Yellow Wiggle, has had to quit the band due to ill health. Clearly this is a sad story, but the magnitude of it is surprising. You see The Wggles out-stripped Nicole Kidman to be Australia's highest earners last year, and are their biggest musical export by miles. Luckily for all their fans, the band has a ready-made replacement in Sam Moran who has been standing in for Greg, most notably on their recent US Tour. Phew. I'm feeling an urge to keep close to this story.

So a nice day out at the zoo was strangely curtailed by a mystery message from home: The lady organising the Adelaide accommodation has been on the phone, she was expecting you today. "Silly cow," I confidently asserted to Matt, "she's got the dates wrong. Bloody Aussie idiots." Brisbane had been hard going but I was intending to get off to a flyer in Adelaide, putting this Aussie right in her place.

Just thought I'd check the flight time so we were definitely at the airport in time tomorrow.

Only it wasn't tomorrow it was today, slap bang in the middle of zoo time. So another 200 quid later we'd committed ourselves to another night in Brisbane and then the only remaining flight that would get us to Adelaide in time to see the start of the Test. Oh yeah, and we were paying for accommodation for tonight in both cities.

Not exactly going to plan so far this trip, maybe Adelaide would be better.

South Australia:
The Festival State

"A cricket tour in Australia would be the most delightful period in your life... if you were deaf."

HAROLD LARWOOD
(ENGLAND FAST BOWLER)

30 November - Arrive Adelaide

So without the need for a responsible adult, we made it to Adelaide. I had got one thing spot-on, the woman who had made the call to the UK was a silly cow after all. Talking us through our digs, she took patronising to a whole new level, making the manner of even someone like Gillian McKeith seem largely down to earth. She could hardly conceal her guffaws when she realised we were there for the cricket. Her parting shot was to shout "Go Aussie," which was pretty ironic as it's exactly what we were thinking.

Now I don't know about you but I usually hate new places upon arrival, and Adelaide was no exception. This is partly around orientation and trying to pig-headedly guess the best places to go, rather than just asking someone or looking it up. Based on initial appearances, shiny, brand-new Brisbane had been replaced by grubby and apparently seedy Adelaide. The first decent sized street (or maybe that should be strip) we encountered was domi-nated by lap-dancing bars. The place had a wild-west kind of feel, or perhaps a traditional old Irish town, with narrow streets and one-storey buildings giving it a slightly dilapidated feel.

Another early moan was that it was pretty damn hot, again, and Adelaide seemed to have its share of flies, and probably Brisbane's share as well.

Anyway, now there was 'work' to do. From an early age I had a great affection for the BBC. This is linked to the fact that I'd never forgiven ITV for going on strike for 11 weeks when I was a kid, so in all major litmus tests, such as *Swap Shop* v *Tiswas* or Cup Final day, the BBC won every time. So I was honoured to be selected as a fan's reporter for BBC Radio Five Live for the Adelaide Test. An added bonus was that I definitely have the face for radio. My only hesitation was purely based around the time of day I would be required to fulfil my wholly unpaid media obligations. Don't get me wrong, I was right up for it, but the problem was speaking on air at around 11am UK time, which equates to half nine at night in South Australia. One thing is clear in a hot climate, you've got to take on liquids at regular intervals, and my concern was that this essential intake would leave me babbling and incoherent by that time. I was keen to avoid bringing shame on myself and my family, in a Sex Pistols meet Bill Grundy kind of way.

The BBC had given me a recording deely and the brief was to get out there and find reasons to be cheerful, as apparently the Brisbane non-performance had left everyone at home a little gloomy about England's prospects. No shit. Being pretty under-whelmed by the city of Adelaide at this stage, the logical place to start seemed to be the cricket ground.

If the city was a metropolitan disappointment after Brisbane, the Adelaide Oval more than made up for it. In fact if you were to close your eyes and imagine an idyllic spot to watch cricket, you would probably picture this place.

On the banks of the River Torrens, the ground has a serenity and stateliness that is a pleasure to behold. On first impressions, this looked like the perfect antidote to the unforgiving and soulless GABBA. Bathed in brilliant sunshine, the Oval was being lovingly prepared upon our arrival, and immediately the grass banks at each end looked perfectly appointed, giving the England fans a chance to congregate and really get behind the team. There were trees to afford natural respite from the punishing sunshine, and the stands were somehow picturesque and modern at the same time. Perfect. Finally the classic Adelaide scoreboard, a series of 'old-school' painted signs and levers and pulleys, had just been restored at a cost of $270,000 and was looking shiny and pristine, as if enthusiastically awaiting the action.

Anyway, enough of that poncy describing stuff, chatting to the England fans it was clear that there were indeed reasons to be cheerful. The main one was that the classic old scoreboard would inevitably bear the name 'Panesar'. Adelaide was notoriously spinner friendly, and it looked as though the Aussies may have made a fatal error in keeping the same 12 from the GABBA and leaving out leg spinner Stuart MacGill. He had been one of England's many nemeses over the years. The general view was that England's demise had been greatly exaggerated and even a Cricket Australia official was prepared to admit he'd had a bet on the tourists at 6-1. The plan was simple for England really, win the toss, bat, bat and then bat some more, then pile the pressure on the occasionally fragile Aussies.

On another positive note, poor old Glenn McGrath was still having problems with his blister. It seemed a bit strange that grouchy old Glennda, the sledging king, could be troubled by something so seemingly trivial. Also interesting were Ricky Ponting's comments; he said that you would have to amputate McGrath's foot to stop him from playing in the Test. Well I was right up for that job, as I'm sure were thousands of other Englishmen in Australia, especially as our batsmen had been beasted by him for the umpteenth time at the GABBA.

If you watch a lot of sport you become obsessive about omens, patterns and coincidences and there was another crumb of comfort to be had here. In the 2005 Ashes Series, England had lost the first test comprehensively; McGrath had taken loads of first innings wickets and England got a hiding. Then before the Second Test, old Glennda picked up a freakish injury, twisting his ankle after stepping on a cricket ball, of all things.

Now maybe a blister was only freakish-ish, but the rest was exactly the same.

So after a day of getting into the Adelaide swing, it was time for my first radio stint, a quick chat on the Matthew Bannister show. It's a bit odd really, you are deliberately not briefed on what you are likely to be asked, presumably so you say stuff off the cuff, rather than thinking too hard about it. After starting off pretty nervously, it all seemed to go off OK, nailed in two minutes and then it was time to go out boozing, probably the best way to gauge if a city really is any good.

After considering the place from a wider perspective, Adelaide is a sprawling area, a town rather than a city really, with loads of parks and churches and maybe feels a bit more like a southern English cathedral town. When in Rome, or even Canterbury, it's important to do as the Romans (or the Cants) do and sample the local brew. This proved to be a lethal but great tipple called Coopers Sparkling Ale, 5.7%ABV, sold in pints (which isn't always the case in Oz) which when you held it up to the light, had the viscosity of a larva lamp. You had as much chance of seeing your hand through a glove than through this stuff.

This newly found relationship served to heal any rift with the place, and I was starting to settle in nicely. Happily sedated and slightly toasted on both sides, it was time to get some sleep, ahead of the Second Test and a sport and alcohol-fest tomorrow.

1 December – Day 1 Adelaide Test
England 266-3

Alcohol is a strange drug really. Socially acceptable and condoned by most governments around the world, this depressant tends to be associated with high sprits and good moods. Whether it has a positive impact on the planet is hugely debatable, but I am sure there are occasions for most people when its absence would completely alter the dynamics of the day.

Friday 1 December 2006 was such a day.

We headed over the river to the Adelaide Oval and there were two major news items to quickly digest. The fact that England had won the toss and decided to bat was very palatable. Once again, following the pattern of the 2005 Ashes Series, England would bat first on a good wicket in the Second Test. Sadly, it was a case of 'pass the Gaviscon Extra Strength' for the other morsel of news. England were unchanged from Brisbane, so no Monty.

If it was a surprise in Brisbane, this news was met with total bemusement by just about everyone here, just what were they thinking? Jimmy Anderson had contributed match figures of 1-195 at the GABBA and had seemed pretty superficial really, brought on as cannon fodder when the Australian batsmen were comfortable and gorging themselves on easy runs against defensive fields. And winning the toss meant that Monty may be an even bigger miss, as he would have bowled in the last innings of the game, when the wicket would presumably be at its worst.

After the insipid display at Brisbane, it almost felt like we were trying to throw the Ashes. Monty isn't a great fielder, nor is he a competent batsman, but he CAN bowl. Australia amassed a combined 804-10 over their two innings at the GABBA. We had to bowl them out twice at some stage to get back into the series. It seemed like a thoroughly defensive move. What made it worse was that this was blatantly obvious to everyone, as palpable as the fact that Michael Jackson's change in appearance isn't entirely down to a skin disease you might say.

Anyway, the majestic Adelaide Oval looked even better when it was packed out and a cloudless sky and fanatical support greeted the opening batsmen in the first session. The hill was heavily populated with England fans, with one of the walkways acting as a natural segregation between the Barmy Army and Australia's sallow imitation, the Fanatics. Once again it was curious to note that loads of the Aussie fans had taches. It seemed that this hairy ailment ha spread across the entirety of this largely barren land. I felt duty bound to inform them of this fashion own-goal as soon as possible.

An early highlight was seeing an Australian attempting to hoof one of the ubiquitous beach balls as hard as he could. The ball went about five yards, his flip-flop at least 20. Great. This incident stood out as major excitement because England's batsmen started with an ultra cautious approach, and had reached only 58-2 at lunch. The Australian fans near us seemed hugely unimpressed, criticising the English approach. It must be great to be an Aussie, not only do you get to support your own very successful team but you also automatically gain the right to critique the play of the opposition as well, perhaps even passing on a few handy hints. Bless. Reminiscent of some Premier League managers of the so-called big clubs you might say.

At lunchtime England were really on the brink, you sensed that if they failed to get the better of the afternoon session, they could be staring down the barrel of a 2-0 score line and the inevitable loss of the Ashes. Coming back from one down against Australia was plausible, from two down was not going to happen.

Then something strange occurred. Slowly but surely England started to get some control, with a dogged partnership between Collingwood and Bell. In fact Bell, who had a bit of a nightmare in the 2005 series, really looked the part. Suddenly it was tea and whilst England certainly hadn't threatened to blow the hinges off the classic scoreboard with a monster scoring rate, they had gone two hours without losing a wicket. Even the bullish Aussies had started to go a bit quiet.

The England supporters on the hill remained standing throughout the day's play and it's pretty hard going in 35 degrees, singing your heart out and staying on your feet. Even tougher for my vertically challenged colleague Matt, who was already bemoaning his calf strains as Day One progressed. The Barmy Army were now in fine voice, singing with real belief the song that was used to lift spirits in Brisbane. It goes to the tune of *Glory, Glory Hallelujah*

The famous England cricket team went one-nil down at Lord's
The famous England cricket team went one-nil down at Lord's
The famous England cricket team went one-nil down at Lord's
And we know what happened next
We won the Ashes at the Oval
We won the Ashes at the Oval
We won the Ashes at the Oval
And we'll win 'em at the SCG-ee-ee

Spirits remained high even when Bell went after tea. This brought in Kevin Pietersen; you know, the one who'd make a great Aussie. He joined Collingwood and they both looked comfortable as they saw England through to the close. Shane Warne's bowling seemed totally innocuous and did nothing more to scupper the 700 wickets bet. In fact, the Australians seemed completely becalmed as Colly, after an agonising 96 in Brisbane, was left stranded on 98 overnight. Hopefully he would get his hundred first thing in the morning and we could press on.

This was a gritty display by England, much better than we could have dreamed of really, especially after the premature capitulation in Brisbane.

Buoyed by this unexpected success, it was time to enjoy more of the biggest day of the year in Adelaide. Not only were they experiencing the first day of the Test, there was also Romario's home debut for Adelaide United and Kylie in concert. Go to all three you say? I should be so lucky. But the plan was definitely to go to the football after the cricket.

At close of play, it was straight to the pub and then attempt to get hold of tickets for the match. The sport formerly known here as wogball, due to its immigrant roots, was enjoying one of the big games of the season, Adelaide United were at home to Melbourne and it was billed as a serious grudge match. Melbourne, league leaders by miles, were captained by one Kevin Muscat, well known by many for his spells in the UK with Palace, Wolves, Millwall and Rangers. His reputation preceded him, he was once dubbed 'the most hated man in football', Muscat was apparently never picked for an Old Firm game at Rangers due to the fixture's volatile nature. Pouring midnight oil on troubled sectarian waters you might say. He'd kept up his track record in the A-League, and the main reason why tonight's game had ill feeling was an incident involving Muscat in the previous meeting. He'd knocked the Adelaide coach over in his technical area, who responded by shaking him warmly by the throat, thereby attracting a five match touchline ban.

But none of this was the big story. 40-year old Brazilian World Cup winner and total legend Romario would make his home debut.

South Australia: The Festival State

The clues should really have been there about the standard of football, a Division Two has-been (or maybe never-was) captains the best team in the country and a 40-year-old retiree was the big story. But you've got to go and have a look haven't you?

We had the good fortune to bump into some local lads who were off to the match so sauntered over with them. Their routine included buying a long-neck (750ml) of the aforementioned Coopers for the walk to the ground. Due to Australia's strict drinking in public laws, this meant wrapping the bottle in some brown paper. As the walk took us through many of Adelaide's parks, another life-long ambition was fulfilled, drinking booze in a park out of a brown paper bag. So proud.

The match was a sell out, but extra tickets went on sale about ten minutes after kick off and we got in just in time to see the second sending-off and a pathetic dive by Romario. In fact, he looked every single one of his 40 years and the standard was pretty poor. My lower division correspondent advised me that it was Conference level at best.

And in common with the cricket fans, the Australians just can't hold down a tune at all. The phrase 'like a cat with barbed-wire being dragged out of its arse' never seemed more appropriate. In an attempt to share the wealth, and indicative of rising alcohol levels, we tried to start a 'we've got Romario' chant, to the tune of *La Donna E Mobile*, or the 'sit down Pinochio' song to you and me. The locals were totally bemused by two people, singing the same words, at the same time, to vaguely the same tune, and just left well alone.

Just after this I got the call from Five Live to have a chat about the day's play. Trying to be sober proved a major challenge. As did being able to respond honestly to the question 'What did Glenn McGrath look like today?' The temptation was to reply with 'what do you think he looked like, he looked like what he is, a really annoying Aussie wanker'. I managed to translate this to something about 'mincing around the outfield' and according to a couple of texts from back home, I'd just about covered up the fact that I'd already been drinking for a good ten hours. My radio nerves had gone from the previous day, but that could be due to the reality that on a drunk-o-meter my reading would be 'almost willing to do karaoke'.

The match petered out with a far superior Melbourne side, seemingly packed with what must be fouth rate Brazilians, cruising to an easy victory. The ground held about 15,000 and it was all quite quaint, nothing like an English atmosphere and much less full-on than the cricket really. The highlight was probably being able to drink while watching the game.

Then it was back into town for more refreshment. I awoke the next day with a hazy recollection of seeing a look-a-like of Lizzie Birdsworth, one of the most grotesque characters from *Prisoner Cell Block H*, but it was all a bit vague really.

2 December – Day 2 Adelaide Test
England 551-6 declared
Australia 28-1

The vague feeling continued as the day started at a snail's pace due to yesterday's excesses. Despite this, it was hard not be hugely boosted by an excellent day for England. But it all started extra fuzzily.

Buying tickets for a 'Test Brekkie' hosted by Terry Jenner, the spin guru who has helped make Shane Warne the amazing bowler he clearly is, had seemed like a brilliant idea on a rainy September afternoon back home. The thought of guzzling loads of fried food, accompanied by free lager at an unearthly hour, was hugely appealing. Alas in sport, timing is vital, and after yesterday's excesses, this really couldn't be worse.

South Australia: The Festival State

Having trudged to the wrong breakfast event, but still nearly getting fed out of sympathy, we managed to arrive around 45 minutes late. Can you see a pattern emerging here? The idea of early morning drinking was wholly repulsive at that time, but the food was welcome if a little hard to keep down.

It was a pretty well organised affair, with several guest appearances, including an interesting insight from Rodney Marsh, the former Aussie wicket-keeper, who was dubbed a traitor for his work at the England Academy. He said that Kevin Pietersen was a very special player and the second best that he had ever worked with. And didn't mention that he'd make a great Australian once. The best he felt was Ricky Ponting. It seemed obvious even then that getting Ponting out twice would be a major challenge for England in this Test, especially as he scored 246-1 on his own at Brisbane.

The highlight was an appearance from Barmy Army trumpeter Billy Cooper, who treated us to Neighbours, Dad's Army (for the Aussie Team) and the Rocky Theme. Billy is also banned from the Adelaide Oval, presumably because he's really good. The event ended with an appearance by Shane Warne and Glenn McGrath, only about an hour before play began. Irritating as it is to report, they both came over as being pretty reasonable. Whisper it quietly but I found myself already grudgingly admiring Warne after his displays of dignity in defeat in England in 2005. With that out of the way, it was time to meander over to the cricket ground. Again the heat was pretty oppressive, with clouds as rare as happy Farepak customers.

England needed to start well, and lo and behold they did. Collingwood nailed his hundred straight away and then England batted and batted. No wickets before lunch meant that England were putting themselves into a really strong position. The Aussie fans went pretty quiet as the honours on and off the pitch went to the visitors.

Ashes To Dust

The Barmy Army were in full voice and again the curiosity/annoyance of some Australians got the better of them as they came over to attempt to disrupt/annoy/engage/goad the England fans. One such local ensconced himself next to me, and happened to be shirtless and covered in yellow body paint. I simply asked him if he had jaundice and he sadly misinterpreted this as an invitation to have a conversation.

He informed me, mainly in words of one syllable, that he was hoping to go to the UK to work in his chosen profession as a plumber, and we got into a conversation about the number of Polish plumbers in the UK. Somewhere in the dark recesses of my mind I knew there were loads of South Korean plumbers in Poland, with free movement of workers and International Trade making the world like one of those slidey number puzzles when there's only one space and it's dead hard to get them sorted. Anyway, that's a major digression. Apparently there are loads of plumbers in Australia. In a feeble attempt to inject some humour (or interest) into our conversation I said 'Loads of plumbers in Australia, not too many brain surgeons though ay.' Not a flicker from my beach bum (maybe that should be plumbum Chemistry fans?) friend.

If things weren't going exactly to plan for me off the pitch, England were totally dictating terms to the Aussies on it. By half way through the day we had 400 on the board and still hadn't lost a wicket. Not one Australian needed to ask us to look at the score-board this time. The milestones came thick and fast with the highlight probably being Paul Collingwood's double century, the first by an Englishman in an Ashes Test in Australia for 70 years, quite an achievement. Brilliant, an indomitable display by a man with more guts than Peter Andre will have when his six-pack finally turns to mush.

That wasn't really the highlight at all. It should have been but it was nice to give the Australians a taste of their own medicine and revel in the misfortune of others. The cheer which greeted the wicketless Shane Warne conceding his hundredth run was every bit as enjoyable. It wasn't just that he hadn't taken a wicket, he seemed to have barely troubled the England batsmen. Just maybe the age-ing Aussies weren't going to last the series. Oh yeah, and it did no harm for the 700 wickets bet either.

'We've got three hundreds on the board' was the song from the Barmy Army, celebrating three figures for Collingwood, Pietersen and Warne. Sweet. The so-called Fanatics were so thoroughly becalmed that they could hardly muster up their favourite chant 'Aussie, Aussie, Aussie, Oi, Oi, Oi.'

Australia's favourite surf-bum Warnie then actually resorted to bowling round the wicket, a wholly negative ploy akin to that employed by Ashley Giles for England, and totally pilloried by the Australians. The blokes (they would definitely have called them-selves that) slagging off England's negativity yesterday were con-spicuous by their absence.

Warne finally got a wicket towards the end but this came at a cost of 167 runs, with Brett Lee and McGrath also clocking up hun-dreds in the runs against column. Their three main bowlers given a chasing, things were turning round nicely. My mate Matt summed it up nicely, for the first time in seven days of cricket, we look like the side that beat them last summer, and they look like the side we beat. He's so deep. Mercifully, nobody was talking about a 5-0 series win any more.

As if to keep my karma in check, I suddenly had a little shudder of recognition from last night. When you start drinking as a young-ster it's a bit alarming the first time you can't remember going up stairs to bed. As you age, this phenomenon creeps into your evening and you realise that autopilot actually sees you into a taxi and then home. Later in life, you forget the last pub you were in. Taking this to its logical conclusion, there will probably be a point in time when you actually forget going out in the first place. My vague Lizzie recollection had now been replaced by a vivid memory that I sung the entire *Prisoner Cell Block H* theme tune to the Birdsworth lookalike outside an Adelaide pub last night. You know the one, 'He used to give me roses, I wish he could again.' Like an umpire giving out a batsman who knows he's nicked it, Matt gives me a casual nod when I ask him for confirmation of this fact. And everything had been going so swimmingly well today.

Speaking of swimming, the England fans took my mind of this embarrassment by with a classic chant of 'you've got the best gay swimmer, in the world'. This is the sort of thing that could monkey around with the macho Australian psyche, although presumably this was a reference to Ian Thorpe and 'gay' in the traditional sense of the word. Kind of happy in his retirement if you will.

Somewhat surprisingly, England declared on 550, and I thought it was maybe a few runs less than expected. Having said that, I asserted to anyone who would listen that this was a positive move. Why not get the Aussies in and then knock them over.

The early dismissal of Langer by the man-mountain Freddie just rammed home this wisdom. Pleasingly Langer had a bit of a row with a fan (probably a South Australia member) as he made his way up the Pavilion steps. Seriously, they get very easily rattled these Aussies. In this case it's the Dad's Army who don't like it up 'em. What England had to do was force home the advantage, there was no way they could lose the game from this situation, it was just a case of doing enough to win it, 19 wickets to go.

A few early breakthroughs in the morning and it could be very tasty.

Continuing the tasty thread, that evening we sat down to eat and for the first time in my life I tried kangaroo meat, this was in a mixed grill situation. It tasted OK, pretty much like the other stuff on the plate really. Then, out of the corner of my eye, I clocked Richie Benaud, total legend, eating on a nearby table. My tactic on seeing famous people is simple; approach them and chat to them as if you've known them all your life. The thing was with Richie, the man who painted my pictures of Australia as a kid (not literally, that was Rolf), I felt like I did know him.

The outcome. Totally bottled it. He looked like he was having a nice time with his (French, I think) wife and another couple so I left him to it. Looks like the Aussies still have some kind of psychological edge over me.

3 December – Day 3 Adelaide Test
England 551-6 declared
Australia 312-5

Legend has it that my old mate Steve Waugh came up with a classic example of sledging in the 1999 World Cup in England. His South African opponent Herschelle Gibbs had just carelessly dropped a crucial catch and the man known as Tugga said: "Son, you've just dropped the World Cup." This was made more profound by the fact that Australia, not South Africa, went on to win it.

As it turns out, Waugh later admitted that what he actually said was "Look, do you realise you've just cost your team the game." This is nowhere near as good but could still constitute humour in a country which revels in the brilliance of Merv Hughes' sledge "Get back in the nets, dickhead." Inspired Merv.

Anyway, back to the original point.

Today just maybe Ashley Giles dropped the Ashes.

England really had Australia in deep trouble, and then let them get away.

The Aussies were already three wickets down with less than 100 on the board, and then came the pivotal moment of the day, perhaps the match and hell who knows, the whole damn series.

The imperious Ponting was looking a little below his best but was still making his way to yet another half century, despite the batting around him crumbling under the pressure of the match situation and some pretty impressive England bowling. People round here have been talking about Ricky Ponting being the best batsmen since Don Bradman, a legend of the game. Bradman is a hugely revered figure, I think even Geoff Boycott described him as "twice as good as any batsman who ever lived". Intriguingly, it only takes a bit of reading about Australian cricket history to learn he was a proper selfish get, Bradman not Boycott obviously.

Whether or not he is the best since the Don, Ponting is the danger man as his 196 and 60 not out in the First Test prove. The moment itself was a bit slow-mo to be honest. Ponting swung the ball to the boundary and you probably expected it to roll to Gilo's feet, an easy single and then get on with it. But there was a bit of excitement in the middle and a sense of anticipation around the ground. A sort of collective intake of breath I guess. I wasn't exactly in the best viewing spot and wholly admire anyone who can actually pick a red cricket ball out of the air and the crowd. Anyway, you knew something important was happening as the ball went to Giles. He made a little jump and put both hands above his head.........then spewed it. Groans all around.

Sometimes you think, well maybe it won't be dead costly and another chance will be along in a minute, but not this time. Sod's law decreed at that moment that Ponting was bound to make a hundred. Just like the mistakes made by fellow controversial inclusion Geraint Jones, every one costs at least 100 runs. This was also extra critical because Hussey and Ponting, the two players at the top of their game, were together at the time.

After that it was attritional stuff really, the Aussie batsmen never looked as comfortable as England yesterday, but their pursuit of our total was pretty relentless. Also without relent, were the

Australians in the ground. As I meander back to my spot, a local accosted me and the conversation went something like this:

Him: Are you a Pom? You can spot the Poms coz they've got too much sunscreen on

Me: Are you an Aussie? You can spot the Aussies coz they're all total gobshites.

No love lost there really. He did have a point though, that Factor 30+ stuff had the consistency of mayonnaise and I was adopting a totally safety-first approach, running the risk of going home even whiter than when I set out.

It was actually a funny day today weather wise, more Stanley Park Oval Blackpool than Adelaide Oval South Australia. It was pretty cool when you were out of the sun and shades were mainly employed to keep your eyes warm on a breezy old day. My paranoia about it being stupidly hot had been an overreaction so far.

Anyway, returning to the England support I am reminded that after Richie-gate last night, Matt and I also bumped into another Ashes legend, this time an English one; Jimmy from the Barmy Army. He was having a quiet-ish drink with his buddies from Oldham. It turns out that Jimmy and his mates are all Latics. Pretty unassuming geezer he was too.

That was Jimmy off duty. Once again today, he was being called upon to rouse the team and the support. The Barmy Army Jimmy ritual goes a bit like this:

1. A few people sing 'Jimmy give us a song'
2. Based on the number of people singing and how long since he last obliged, Jimmy will probably ignore this request.
3. A few more people will sing 'Jimmy give us a song'
4. Jimmy will get on the shoulders of his mates/minders

5. Most people will sing 'He's only got one song'
6. Then Jimmy will call for hush
7. Then he will start the 'Everywhere we go-oh' song
8. Everyone will join in, culminating in "Barmy Army, Barmy Army" repeat to fade (about 15 minutes later)

The players really needed this support today. They were battling away well in the field, but just not having much luck. The previously maligned Jimmy Anderson had the new Don Bradman in real trouble at times, but it didn't stop the Aussie captain making yet another hundred, as he and Hussey put on nearly 200 for the 4th wicket. Two wickets late in the day gave England a much-needed boost, both taken by Hoggard who claimed all four wickets today.

I must admit to not having previously been a big fan of Hoggy, probably to do with the fact that I am a Lancastrian living in Yorkshire. His figures of 0-60 off four overs during a Roses Twenty20 game at Headingley had caused me great hilarity. Not that he'd be bothered in the slightest, but he really won me over today. His wholehearted efforts kept England in charge of the game, even though a draw now seemed by far the most likely outcome.

The only way to prevent this seemed to be for England to take early wickets tomorrow. They needed this as much as I needed a night off the booze, both pretty unlikely but certainly something worth striving for.

4 December – Day 4 Adelaide
England 551-6 declared and 59-1
Australia 513

A good way of getting to know someone quite quickly is to spend some time in the same living space as them. My time with

South Australia: The Festival State

Matt is coming to an end, he's off home after this Test, and I will honestly be sad to see him go. That said, we've lived at a pace that has been hard to maintain. Last night his brilliance shone through again. We had a night in, trying some kind of vain attempt to slow things down a little.

Our ideas on the agenda differed and it turned out that our quiet one was an Indian takeaway, a few beers (Coopers of course) and a couple of bottles of wine. That'll sort it.

So the night off the ale failed, just like England's quest to get early wickets. More ominously, the strange looking but stupidly destructive Adam Gilchrist helped himself to a half-century. One of England's major successes in the previous series was restricting the free-scoring wicket keeper to a handful of runs. If he hits top form, or hits his straps as they say here, whatever that means, we've got real problems.

Another player who achieved very little in England was Michael Clarke. He looks like a bit of a golden boy of Australian cricket does Clarke, seemingly an automatic pick and possibly destined to be captain one day. The fact that he managed to rack up a century today is the final confirmation that the pitch is pretty benign. It also presented a chance to experience another speciality in Australia, parochialism. Having taken a bit of respite from the hot afternoon sun, we found ourselves sitting with a father and son combo. They were spot on and we had a proper good conversation. They hated Michael Clarke with a passion, partly fuelled by a New South Wales bias in the Aussie cricket team and wider cricket establishment. The story also goes that young Master Clarke was born with a silver bail in his mouth, and was still in single figures age wise when he was bought his first bowling machine. No idea if it's true, nice tale though.

This reminded me of my previous trip to Melbourne, when one particular local I met hated New South Welshman Mark Waugh, as he had been given Victorian Dean Jones' spot in the Aussie Test team. He must be used to getting displaced old Deano, having recently lost his commentary job for referring to the bearded South African Amla as a terrorist. Anyway, this Victorian wanted to join in with the Barmy Army song lampooning Waugh for taking cash from an Indian bookmaker in return for team information. Sadly, being an Australian, the complex lyrical content was far too much for him.

Having taken respite from the blazing sun, it was time to get back to the hill. The game was going nowhere really, as the Aussies made their way towards England's total. We then got chatting to a family from Wigan who had emigrated to Oz and were living in the Barossa Valley, with the hubby working for Wolf Blass. After a while it seemed an appropriate time to say..........

Me: Is there a B&Q in Wigan?
Wiganer (enthusiastically): Yeah, and we've got Asdas as well.

Most will know that the required response here is, 'No, there's a 'W', an 'I' etc etc. It just shows that the ability to let jokes go flying over your head is something you can learn when you emigrate, maybe it forms part of the entry requirements, who knows?

The highlight on the pitch was the continued efforts of Matthew Hoggard. The Barmy Army's hero, I think this is due to his down to earth manner and his slight eccentricity. He is also a total 100%-er and I've got some indistinct recollection around the fact that he hates Matthew Hayden. Anyway, Hoggy steamed in to bowl a total of 42 overs in the innings and took a hugely creditable 7-109. This looks even better when you notice that the rest of the side took three wickets for over 400 runs.

It was really hot again out there, and this seemed to make the authorities a bit tetchier than usual. Again, the South Australian police had contented themselves mainly with ejecting Australians, but today they took decisive action to quell a real danger. The problem was that there was a crocodile in the crowd, surely something serious had to be done. Granted, it was inflatable, and it was wearing a T-shirt bearing the slogan 'Pommie Crocs Rule' but the police were right to be cautious. Thankfully the dangerous animal was ejected with the maximum of fuss.

As for the game, England had to endure Clarke and Warne putting on over a hundred for the 7th wicket, which makes the game safe for them. Happily England then rattled through the tail, which they couldn't do in Brisbane, and removed the last four wickets for a handful of runs. And controversial selection Jimmy Anderson at least picked up a wicket, getting McGrath to wrap up the innings.

Having gone for a wander at the changeover, I bumped into an Aussie lad I had been chatting to a couple of days earlier. He was one of the culprits in the moustache stakes, although you had to admit that his was glorious, embodying the spirit of David Boon, Merv Hughes and Lord Kitchener with a magnificent facial growth, the sort of thing that would probably have to go into quarantine for six weeks if you wanted to go abroad. So after complimenting him on the thing, I had to ask why so many Aussies were sporting the mouser. The real reason was around the 'Movember' campaign, where men (and presumably some women) were growing a tache to raise money for The Prostate Cancer Charity. Thankfully I'd not made too many smart arsed comments about it. Phew.

England had just over an hour to bat and it was hard to gauge what their approach should be really. A declaration at any stage would appear to be suicidal on such a good wicket, so we were in one of those phoney war phases again, with the players partly going through the motions in what was a nailed on draw. The sequence in terms of the number of wickets falling each day had been 3, 4, 4 and 5, so the chance of a clatter of wickets on Day five was pretty much zero.

Another sequence of numbers was cause for English concern. The openers again failed to put on a significant partnership, adding a stand of 31 to their previous efforts of 28, 29 and 32. It was obvious they were getting a start and then letting it go, with the innocuous looking Stuart Clark often proving to be a problem. If we were going to turn the series around, this area had to improve.

As we left the ground, possibly still a bit deflated that England had to settle for a draw having largely bossed the game, we were accosted by a few smartly dressed old Aussie gents who wanted to know all about us and help by showing us the best places to go drinking. Really nice geezers they were, so what came next was a bit of a surprise.

We were being guided past loads of pubs which were heaving with thirsty cricket fans until the crowds had thinned out a bit, and we reached one which didn't look too bad. Our antipodean tour guide then said, "'you don't wanna go in there mate, that's a wogs pub. Yeah, that ones owned by the wogs." This was a bit of a shock really, like I said, PC World this place ain't. What's more, he seemed quite proud of this information, and must have managed to use the word 'wogs' on about five occasions in a minute. It seems likely that he meant no major malice with this label, but it was very odd to hear it used at all, and then so liberally. Ho hum. Not that I'm likely to experience it but the Aussie workplace must be a crazy scene.

Anyway, we nailed a few drinks before retiring back to our digs to double and treble check our flight details. After missing an interal flight by a day, the chances of one of us getting to New Zealand, and the other making it back to Manchester, seemed pretty remote. We also decided that as the game was pretty much over, it didn't really matter if we were a few minutes late for Day five.

5 December – Adelaide Test Day 5
England 551-6 declared and 129
Australia 513 and 168-4
Australia won by 6 wickets

I've been mugged once in my life and it's a strange old sensation really. You feel like you should have seen it coming, rack your brains for what you could have done to avoid it and are left with a general feeling of emptiness and violation. That's how it feels right now.

Even reflecting back it is hard to believe this has happened. England really blew it big time, and that's pretty much the Ashes gone.

It seemed like an injustice this morning that despite being totally in charge of the game from lunchtime on the First Day, England were probably the only team who had a chance of losing it, such are the vagaries of Test Match cricket. Of course it was a possibility, but it seemed so remote that it was hardly worth considering.

The fact is that the Aussies are persistent and ruthless, and if they see any kind of opportunity they greedily seize it with both hands. And it appeared that England just got scared. It would take a brave and stupid man to predict anything other than an Australian Ashes victory, and I'm neither of those things. Well maybe stupid for blowing my dough on this ill-fated trip.

And it was supposed to be so easy.

There were no clues whatsoever as we meandered to the ground, taking in the beautiful surroundings for the last time, not really worrying about the time and getting into position for about 11:15. Surprise, surprise, nothing much had happened and no wickets had fallen. Warne was bound to get a long bowl today and was quickly into the action. They were a few alarms and loads of noise from the Aussie fielders, but nothing out of the ordinary there to be honest.

Not long after that Strauss was out, appearing to get yet another dodgy decision, but he'd been in no sort of form anyway, and England had managed to clock up 550 in the first innings without a major contribution from him. It did make you wonder how many Test wickets Warne would have if you took away the dodgy decisions, but there you go. The only real worry at this stage was that England were getting a bit bogged down, adding to any potential pressure by failing to keep the scoreboard ticking over.

Then the moment which seemed to change the game.

Bell and Collingwood, who'd both batted well in the first innings, were involved in the kind of crass run out which drives everyone mental. Possibly conscious of the snail's pace run rate, Colly set off for a quick single, his team-mate didn't and the ensuing mess led to Bell's end (leave it). It was an archetypal dismissal for a team that was petrified of the situation.

Worse was to follow very soon after. Having faced only four balls, the super confident Kevin Pietersen attempted an extravagant sweep and was bowled round his legs. It was now mid-way through the morning session and suddenly England found themselves 73-4, with five hours to go in the day and a fragile lead of a meagre 111, a significant number in cricket terms and a further portent of doom.

It was hard to work out exactly what was going on. This batsman's paradise had suddenly appeared to become the wicket from hell. England had scored just 16 runs from 14 overs, and contrived to lose three wickets in that period of play.

Anyone who watches any sport will know how this feels. You can see the disaster looming. Your sporting sixth sense kicks in and you get a bad, bad feeling about it. There are some occasions when your team flirts with danger but it actually works out just fine in the end. Then it's almost fun that you cheated defeat, and you can confidently inform your rivals that you were not concerned in the slightest, and had the utmost faith in your team, knowing full well that they would pull through in the circumstances.

It didn't seem too likely on this occasion.

By now the Aussies were going absolutely mental in the field, they'd got the scent of blood in their nostrils and wanted more. They were literally appealing after every ball, with oohs, aahs and catch its coming from all quarters. One gent near me sagely remarked that it appeared the Australians were appealing for a mythical 11th mode of dismissal - 'Bat Before Wicket'.

What England needed was a partnership of some kind, just to see them through to lunch time, get in the dressing room, get sorted. Then the distinctly average Brett Lee, who in fairness was bowling well over 90mph, got Freddie out and we were right in the mire. Now I'll concede that I've never played Test Match cricket, but to me Lee is a pretty ordinary bowler, he just bowls fast. He'd been slapped around for four an over in the First Innings, yet suddenly he looked unplayable as well.

By lunch England were 89-5, having scored an unbelievable 30 runs in 28 overs. They were scared, and so were all the England fans. Lunch break was an uncomfortable 40 minutes, but you still clung to the hope that the break would do England good, and a sense of order and reality would be restored after a bit of sustenance.

No such luck.

The hapless Jones was out to an awful looking shot, the delivery looked like it might have been a wide if he hadn't stretched to reach it. Then came Gilo, a man selected for his superior batting, with a classic chance to make amends for dropping Ponting on Day Three. Not a sniff. 14 balls and no runs later, he was back in the hutch too.

Hoggard and Harmison did OK, seeing off 52 deliveries between them as time became a major factor in the game. At the other end Paul Collingwood must have wondered what the hell was going on. The problem for England was that he was totally becalmed and had stopped scoring runs as well. The tourists were making rabbits caught in headlights appear totally unruffled and unconcerned by their illuminated plight.

Then came Jimmy Anderson, England's last man. This was excruciatingly painful to watch from the hill, but somehow Jimmy was surviving quite well and as tea approached it looked like England may just be doing enough to save it. Australia would already need to score at around four an over, not exactly straightforward, and maybe the wicket was now playing tricks. The Barmy Army imitated the excessive appealing of the Australians, voicing a massive spoof 'howzat' every ball as the Australians got more and more desperate. Jimmy had lasted ten priceless overs when another mocking appeal went up for a ball that looked like it was missing by miles. It's stating the obvious to say the entire Aussie team also went up as one.

OUT.

So, after another apparently shocking decision, Australia needed 168 to win in 30-odd overs. In most circumstances this would be easily do-able, but it was a high-pressure situation. If we could get bowled out on the cheap, why couldn't Australia?

The 20-minute break was pretty much unbearable. The general view was that we had completely blown it, but this next couple of hours was crucial. It's a curiosity of cricket that there are so many playing conditions, nobody was certain how long we had to play. Frantic speculation followed. Overtime had been necessary on every evening but there had been a cut off point. Could this ruling save England? No. You played until all the overs were completed, and bad light was as likely as a shy and retiring Aussie fielder. With the required rate being what it was, the next two hours would decide everything, it was either going to be 2-0 or 1-1, and a famous victory for one of the teams.

If there was any doubt about this it was dispelled immediately as Australia set off in a major hurry. There was quite a lot of optimism as England had them 33-2 in the 6th over. Both wickets had been greeted by pandemonium, the sort of the reaction unusual at cricket, and old football terrace style of going mental. Then Ponting and Hussey, who were becoming a real pain in the arse if the truth be told, came together and took the game away from England.

The single biggest incident that summed up England's paucity of ideas was bringing on Kevin Pietersen to bowl. Nothing against KP, but when the Aussies needed wickets, they turned to a man with nearly 700 to his name, we chucked it to a bloke with just the one. Pathetic really.

There was a slight glimmer of hope when Giles got Ponting and Martyn quickly followed, but hopes were quickly dashed. It seemed unbelievable that we'd all spent five days there and that this was the outcome. There had really been no clues at all.

We also had to endure the derision of the Aussies when Pietersen's overthrows led to the batsmen being gifted a '7', and the picture of Freddie on the big screen, looking on the verge of tears. We all were.

The England fans' support of their cricket team seems to pretty much border on unconditional love. The Barmy Army was spawned when England were pretty rubbish so no-one expects the team have a divine right to win. There is probably a pretty realistic acknowledgement that a few things went in our favour in the last Ashes Series too, so it wasn't like we expected a walk in the park in Australia.

One or two fans turned on the players now and this seemed very unusual. They were probably well within their rights to do so, and it's not as if the players can hear their criticisms anyway. These views went unchallenged. I remember an incident at Goodison Park once when two blokes virtually started fighting based on negative comments about David Unsworth. Well Unsy would have needed bionic hearing to pick up on the grief he was getting anyway.

The England fans have every right to be disappointed though. No one is suggesting the players have thrown the game or any-thing, but this is a sickening and more importantly probably termi-nal defeat. We all know it.

The Aussie fans who we all feel we've out-sung, out-thought and out-witted for five days, will have the last laugh. And why wouldn't they. This is a spectacular victory for a sporting team that pretty much unites their nation.

Rubbish.

No idea if the England players came over to salute the sup-port. I doubt it. When the last run was hit, it was time to leave. Enough bad medicine for one day.

There is nothing more to say. This feels like it should be the end of my account of the Ashes really, we've blown it today.

Gutted.

New Zealand:
The Eldorado State

"The proper means of increasing the love we bear our native country is to reside some time in a foreign one."

William Shenstone
(English Poet)

6 December - Arrive Auckland

Funnily enough, a few drinks were consumed last night, but nowhere near enough to take away the bitter taste of defeat. What happened yesterday is still hard to take and hard to believe, but it happened.... so there you go.

The first thing to do today was get up, get sorted, get packed and get down to the airport. Matt was flying back to Brisbane, then off home. I was heading to NZ to see a couple I know.

As we tried to make our way through Australia's rigorous security checks, it was time to go our separate ways. Quite an emotional moment to be honest, as me and Matt really got on well on this trip and had a proper laugh. Usually when you're on a lads holiday, there are loads of you, but even though there was only us two, it still went off as well as possible. The two defeats weren't good, despite what Nelson Mandela's chiropodist might say, and they've probably taken a bit of the shine off the trip.

Although I know one or two people who are out here, and have got to know quite a few more, it was still sad to see my mate go home. This is the bloke whose holiday I sabotaged with my grand plans, who had waited around while I'd laboured as a ham radio reporter. This was my drinking buddy, the geezer who had voraciously eaten and boozed with me for 16 days solid. Our cameraman, our celeb spotter, the guy who had taught me that a quiet night in meant only drinking to a bit of excess.

It was hard to know what to say as we stood in silence. I felt duty bound to break the peace:

"Thank fuck you're going home, I couldn't live like this much longer."

Not a flicker of emotion from Matt, who simply added, 'I was just about to say the same thing, can't wait to get back.'

We vowed to watch a one-dayer together when I got back and try to re-create a day at the GABBA. This could be achieved by turning the heating on full blast, drinking weak lager and getting some local ASBOs to heckle us constantly. It'd be just like the real thing.

And then I was on my own.

I couldn't stop reflecting on what had gone on at the Adelaide Oval the day before. It probably sounds glib but when your team suffers a monumental defeat you go through some kind of grieving process. I was now entering the acceptance phase.

Another curiosity is that I actually felt pleased to have been there to witness it. That may appear odd, but maybe some people will know what I mean. The alternative – had I been at home – would have been as follows when Day five was about to start

New Zealand: The Eldorado State

1. Go to bed safe in the knowledge that a draw was on the cards, wondering if there was a tiny chance of a miraculous England victory.

2. Wake up in the middle of the night, just to double check that the nailed on draw was still totally nailed on.

3. Get a major shock when I found out the score. Stick the radio on, and drift in and out of sleep, occasionally awoken by the sound of excitable commentators, probably Aussies, doing their nut as the latest wicket went down.

4. Maintain this half sleep through a feeling of being dazed and confused, wondering if it had all been some bad dream

5. Get up as the Aussies chase their miniscule target

6. Get ready for work, swearing constantly and occasionally celebrating each wicket, clutching at those tenuous straws in a losing cause.

7. As the death knell sounded, drive to work in the cold, totally strung out and grouchy as hell for the day ahead.

What a feeling.

At least by being there you get to see the full horror unfold. As soon as the run-out happened, there was a bad vibe around the place and an air of inevitability about everything that followed. Australia are the best side in the world for many, many reasons, but the biggest is that they are ruthlessly professional. The fact that England were more single-minded and merciless in the 2005 series, was a major reason for their Ashes victory.

But at Adelaide England got scared by the situation, Australia excited by it.

Another angle I contemplate is maybe, just maybe, it was a bit of an honour to see a master craftsman like Warne at work. He described it as the best ever victory he'd been involved in, so maybe I can look back with pride one day and say 'I was there'. Bowling Shane.

As we left the ground the Aussies were understandably jubilant, gleefully pointing out that the series scoreline was now indeed 2-0. Clever stuff. In fairness to them, the cricket fans of Adelaide had been nowhere near as irritating as their Brisbane counterparts, and this was truly a remarkable victory. Their incessant and witless chants still pissed me off, although perhaps not as much as the speed of England's timorous capitulation.

So now to New Zealand, hopefully to take my mind off the cricket. My imminent destination instantly had one massive advantage over my previous location; it wasn't full of Aussies.

At the airport I saw a few familiar faces who would be making their way to Perth and getting ready for the next Test. It felt quite liberating to be heading off in a different direction really. Upon arrival in Auckland, I was barracked by an immigration officer, who told me that touring round Australia to watch the cricket sounded like 'a pretty stupid thing to do.' It seems that the ability to state the bleeding obvious is one that transcends the Tasman Sea.

I had one night in Auckland before heading down to see my mate, so didn't really have time to go through the rigmarole of hating the place. That said, on the approach it did look like a bit of a dump in places really, and had the appearance of a British city, some nice bits, some nasty bits.

One surprise was the distinct difference in accents between Aussies and Kiwis. I'd always assumed it was pretty much the same, but the disparity was pretty stark. When I asked for directions from my hotel to find somewhere to eat, I was informed that I needed to walk straight out of the hotel and then 'go lift at the intersuction.' This left (or should that be lift) me pretty cold, so I decided to have a night in.

Reading the in-room blurb, I realised that Auckland had a place called 'Minus-5', a bar made of ice. This would have been a quality antidote to Adelaide's searing heat, but I quickly realised that I didn't have the clobber. Not much point turning up there in my T-shirt and pirate keks. It would have been nice to visit though.

Maybe it's just me, but I felt guilty being in another city and doing absolutely nothing about seeing much more than the four walls of a hotel. It's probably a curiosity of human nature that even when we are relaxing, it is still normal to heap pressure on our-selves. It was already apparent that I wasn't going to see much of Australia really. When people in Adelaide asked where we'd been around Brisbane it was a case of the Zoo, the bar and the GABBA, and that was it. Not exactly Ray Mears, but who wants to eat lichens anyway?

Enough. Time to work out how the hell you get those rubbish itchy blankets off the bed (does anybody like them?), and then get some kip before another flight in the morning.

I realised that finally I had reached my Utopia, something I'd been yearning for over a period of more than two weeks. Fantastic. A booze-free day.

7 December – Arrive Nelson

So it's straight down to the airport to get a flight to Nelson, which is at the top of the South Island, 90 minutes from Auckland. As promised, the views were inspiring, with the snow topped sight of Mount Taranaki breathtaking.

It's immediately obvious that New Zealand is a seriously mountainous country, in fact, according to the elder of the Michael Clarke haters, if you flattened it out it would be the same size as Australia. The plane ride was pretty intimate, there's no alternative on a 30-seater, and the lady in the next seat to me also had a bit of hatred in her. She was focussed on the Rugby World Cup in France in 2007. Basically she was desperate for the All Blacks to give the Frenchies their comeuppance, still smarting from the Rainbow Warrior incident of ages ago. I was ashamed to admit I'd forgotten all about that.

In addition to the guest appearances on BBC Radio Five Live, the other thing I had been doing (more unpaid stuff I'm afraid) was a blog on behalf of the Barmy Army for Yahoo Sports. This meant writing around 300 words at the end of each day to sum up what had occurred. After my experience at the GABBA, I had already upset the Aussie readership with one of two playful jibes at their expense.

It didn't take much to wind them up to be honest. Waking up each morning to check how much abuse I had received was a funny feeling really. What I found really heartening was the support I was getting from people I knew, and some that I didn't. Really touching that and a good way of keeping in contact with old mates.

The Adelaide capitulation had given my antipodean 'friends' a chance to strike back, and the flight provided a great opportunity to read through their comments. I was described as bitter, sub-human, numbnuts and a big-mouthed slob. Not bad. I was also given some clear instruction such as grow up, stop whingeing and get over it, which I was starting to do. You would have thought gracious winners would have something better to do with their time - but maybe not. You've got to admire their patience and dogged determination though; it takes ages to get on the internet in Australia.

Anyway, the smallest plane I had ever been on touched down safely and I soon met my mate. We visited the beach on a place called Rabbit Island, and it was great to be out of the city and in some wide-open space. By the time we left, it was getting dark and it would have been nice to see if we could catch any England batsmen in our headlights, but there were none around.

There's a lot of room in New Zealand, a truly spacious country. In the evening we met up with a couple of Yorkshire lads my mate knew and the emotive issue of emigration/immigration inevitably cropped up. One of the lads had emigrated, taking his wife and kids with him, without ever having visited the country in advance. Now we all do impulsive – and arguably stupid – things, like jacking your job in and following a rubbish cricket team on the other side of the world, but this seemed right 'out there'. My view on whether you like a place is that it's an intuitive process, some gut feeling that you can't quite put your finger on.

New Zealand is a beautiful place. But so are the Lake District and the Highlands of Scotland, still not sure I'd want to live there, though. This particular individual's palpable homesickness wasn't a huge surprise. It now occurred to me that ex-pat Brits come to Australia and New Zealand searching for some kind of El Dorado. The reason of a better upbringing for their kids is often cited, and admittedly this rationale is pretty tough to argue with. In fact there are so many poms (hate that term) over here that several of the kids are starting school in a class with more English kids than Kiwis. The town of Brightwater in New Zealand has been re-named 'Britwater' by the locals for that very reason.

With this honourable exception, the ex-pats in New Zealand seemed to be happy with their choices in general, but the ones I'd spoken to and observed in Oz, most particularly at the cricket, seemed a little less secure with their choices. This represents a chance to make some sweeping generalisations and to categorise groups of people in a wholly arbitrary and unnecessary way.

EX-PATS IN OZ

Group 1 – Über-Poms
The general vibe at the cricket is that the England fans support their team fervently, but this rarely spills over into fighting/hassle.

Some Aussies come over to goad the English, but are often too drunk to fight. This group of ex-pats appear to be sick of taking verbals from the locals and being in a foreign land has served to fuel their Englishness. So they combine the worst qualities of the two. They are English, aggressive, drunk and right up for it.

Group 2 – Humans

These people keep their English accent, and maintain an English-ness to their outlook. They often try to sell the emigration dream to you, but this seems partly to justify their decision to do it, partly to eulogise about what a great place it is. They still support England, and get on fine with the Aussies, whilst occasionally finding their patter a bit lame. The Humans will watch as much English football as they can, but also adopt their local football, Aussie rules or Rugby League team, and support them too.

Group 3 – Brucey Britons

This mob actually forget they were ever English, and adopt all things Australian. It MAY be acceptable to support Australia against any other team, but to support them against your country of birth should probably be treasonable, pretty handy that we've got the same Queen really. These people also seem to have pretty extreme views on UK immigration, amused by the fact that we are inheriting people from former Eastern European countries. A subset of this group - rare but despicable - are those ex-pat Englishmen who actually change sides dependant upon which team has the upper hand. Shameful.

So there.

Back to New Zealand. My fellow drinkers and I ended the evening in an English theme pub of all places. There was a roaring fire and a couple of pints of Boddingtons went down nicely. It seemed pretty bizarre to be in a place like this, 13,000 or so miles away from home, but kind of comforting too. The world sure is a tiny place, although Matt should just about have made it home by now.

I probably needed to start thinking about all things cricket again, but upon surfing the internet, not the easiest thing to do out in the sticks in New Zealand, I stumbled across a good news story. Sam Moran made a successful debut (or daybooooo as they say in Australia) for The Wiggles in place of Greg Page. Apparently he wore the yellow skivvy (which, according to reports, is a shirt) with great authority. Thank God for that; now I'll sleep tonight.

8 December

Turning to the cricket news again, there was a lot of information to digest. As Sod's Law would have it, the only Aussie batsman we seemed to have sussed, Damien Martyn, had suddenly decided to call it a day and retire from all cricket with immediate effect. This seemed like a mysterious decision, especially as the next and probably Ashes-clinching Test will take place at his home ground in Perth.

It is easy to rush to the conclusion that he decided to fall on his sword (leave it) and jump before he was pushed, but even that isn't clear.

Another player who won't see the Ashes light of day is Michael Vaughan. So much for my fitness assessment from the nets in Brisbane. The long-term prognosis must seriously question him ever playing for England again. So any potential batting selection headache is now gone. Trescothick's flown home, so the top six pretty much pick themselves for the rest of the series.

There is also a Test series going on over here in NZ, but to say it is lower profile than the Ashes is a serious understatement, perhaps in the vain of 'Houston, we've got a problem'. That's a

NASA reference not a Bobby Brown one by the way. Part of the problem here is that the home Black Caps are playing Sri Lanka for the third consecutive summer. The papers are comparing the crowds to those for The Ashes. Yesterday the attendance at the 37,000 capacity Jade Stadium was a paltry 1,185. Kiwi journo Geoff Longley summed it up nicely with his quip, 'a crazed gunman could have burst into the ground, cut loose and hit nobody.'

I hadn't realised that the Kiwis referred to their team as The Black Caps quite so zealously. They love that sort of thing here, stemming presumably from the famous All Blacks. In fact they also have these collective names for various sporting teams; Silver Ferns, Black Sticks, White Ferns and my own personal favourite, the basketball team is known as the Tall Blacks.

It was more about tall orders for the England players, as they get back to business tomorrow in their final state game of the tour against Western Australia. Monty is sure to be selected for this one, giving him a chance to press his claims for a start in the Third Test. The way England's selections have gone so far this tour, he'll probably take all 20 wickets and still not get a spot.

It would be nice to think that England could record their first victory of the tour. The WA team will feature Adam Voges who has been called up as the surprise replacement for the retired Martyn. Voges is a right-handed batsman, who Ricky Ponting apparently preferred over the other more established left-handers. The reason? To combat the wicked spin of Ashley Giles. Who said Ricky hasn't got a sense of humour? Well, nearly all of us last summer, but it just shows how wrong you can be.

Away from the cricket, I witnessed more spectacular New Zealand scenery today, and very verdant it is too. Undulating hills and valleys as far as the eye can see; tall trees, clear springs, truly a well-preserved nation. Based on the lifestyle and the limited experience I have of both Australia and New Zealand, I'd conclude that

New Zealand: The Eldorado State

New Zealand is to Australia what maybe Ireland is to England. More laid back, more unspoilt.

The evening saw us head into Nelson for a few drinks and eventually to see a band. Their music was a blend of several different genres, with a bit of ska, reggae and probably funk chucked in there as well. Not really my bag, but quite entertaining nonetheless. They were called the Taliband and the show also featured Osama Bin Lager. Enough said.

It was pretty noticeable for a Friday that the night out was a quiet one. I'm sure it differs elsewhere in the country, but the conclusion had to be drawn that New Zealand was a great place to bring up your kids, but maybe not amazing for a night out. The evening was livened up by a story about one of the ex-pats who had laid some decking for a local. This no-nonsense Yorkie was told by the Kiwi to "sit on mi dick and I'll give you a sausage." Thankfully, after much confusion, he got the BBQ jist of it in the end.

My stay in Nelson ends tomorrow, then it's back to Auckland to look at a different four hotel room walls, before plunging back to the action.

9 December − Arrive Auckland

Over in Perth, the England players were continuing to confound the selection policy (if we have one) with Anderson, Mahmood, Panesar and Harmison all taking wickets. Harmy significantly picked up the wicket of Adam Voges.

Voges appears to be competing for a place in the side with Andrew Symonds. The English-born Symonds, if selected, will give us more ammunition to goad the Aussies with, even if it is in a losing cause.

Irrespective of what happens in the two-day game against WA, and how the hell we are supposed to get a win in two days is beyond me, changes have to be made. Monty coming in must be a cert, with Sajid Mahmood standing a decent chance of selection ahead of Jimmy Anderson. An alternative would be to play both the Lancashire lads and omit the clearly out of sorts Steve Harmison, but loyalty is the watchword of the England management set-up; he'll play even if he's phoning home on the field between overs.

There is a third way. The Perth wicket used to be the fastest in the world, but has slowed loads over the years apparently, so two spinners is a possibility. England may go in with one and half, and that's being kind to Gilo based on his displays so far.

That reminded me that some English lads were telling us a story about sharing a lift with Ashley Giles on the day of the dropped Ponting chance. Apparently the 'King of Spain' was very magnanimous and simply stated: "I know I fucked it up."

My final act in Nelson was an afternoon hike up to the dead centre of New Zealand, (not a cemetery) which was a scenic walk up to a relatively steep incline and you had to say that the views were spectacular. In fact, everywhere you looked in this country the views were spectacular. You could see why Hollywood producers choose this place to film their nerd movies for the types who used to play Dungeons and Dragons as kids instead of getting out and playing sport or learning how to smoke or something.

At the summit two middle-aged ladies congratulated my friend on his decision to choose New Zealand over Australia as the place to settle his family. 'Bitter wither' they cited. Couldn't agree more, it had been great to get away from the Aussie heat for a few days. But that respite was just about over.

I said goodbye to my gracious hosts and it was time to head back to rejoin the Tour. First it was one of those remote controlled planes, well a 30-seater, back to Auckland. It seemed wholly appropriate to get me back into the swing of watching cricket in Australia, that the main road from Auckland airport is called Hugh

Watt drive. Hearing the Aussies sing it usually is a case of "Hugh Watt, Hugh Watt, Hugh Watt Hugh Watt Hugh Watt."

A stupidly early start tomorrow for a 7am flight (well three flights in total) to meander my way across the Tasman to the vast landmass that is Australia. Still I figure I'll maybe take a sneaky peek at the Manchester derby, live on my hotel TV at 01:45. Definitely maybe.

Ashes To Dust

At the GABBA with Bella, Kath and Kim, sharing that 'I said I was going to wear the yellow (not gold) and green sombrero' moment.

With some English wrestling legends. Check out the tight clothing, face paint and scary expression on the one in the middle.

There were some weird sights at the GABBA, none more so than Doctor Steve, the English eccentric (middle), who joined me, Matt (second left) and the Queensland fun police.

These English lads decided to help reinforce the stuffy English stereotype with a City Gent look. Their cut-off suit keks are sadly out of shot.

Michael Vaughan having a net at Brisbane during the First Test. Just about as close as he got to the Ashes frontline.

Day Four at Brisbane and the tour already appears to be taking its toll on both me and Tuffers.

Showing Skippy, who is bigger than he looks on TV, just who's boss round here. Check out the big ears, gormless expression and long flat nose on the one on the left.

Day Five at Brisbane. Barmy support featuring the optimistic umbrella (as seen on the front cover) despite bright overhead conditions.

One down, four to go. The GABBA's coloured seats make the 'Spot the Aussie' competition a little more difficult.

Possibly the lithe Jimmy's first meal of the tour, note the white jeans still in pristine condition.

Steve Irwin RIP. Luckily there's a veritable conveyor belt of successors, willing to goad crocs to the point of attack.

Crikey, how high can you go? Not very high at all judging by these two sylph-like athletes.

Trying and miserably failing to look as cool as Michael Holding in Adelaide. Check out one of Adelaide's vast green expanses, in the foreground on the left, in front of the park.

Bumping into Sky Sports News' Tim Abrahams for the umpteenth time. You've got to feel for Tim, who has one of THE worst jobs in the world.

With former England Ashes hero Gladstone Small. Yes, I got my hands on his shoulders and yes, he is rock solid.

Getting dangerously close to Jimmy's armpit. He's only got one song (and outfit) you know.

The quaint spectacle that is the Hyundai A-League, Adelaide United v Melbourne Victory. If ever you go, take your boots, you might just get a game.

The hill at Adelaide; featuring England fans amusing themselves with a huge flag as the Test peters out into an inevitable draw.

POMMIE CROCS RULE. Thankfully, this extraordinarily dangerous specimen was removed by the fun police. Strewth!

Bowling to the statue of Don Bradman in Adelaide.
He hit it out of the park.

Taking respite on a beautiful beach in New Zealand,
the only place it was now safe to wear an England shirt.
Don't even ask, it's sea water alright.

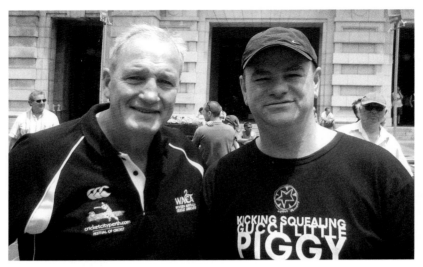

In Perth with Jen Embuwee, England spin legend
and genuinely nice geezer.

Out on the tiles with my mate Bumble.
Probably the highlight of the tour.

Me and Gatt using the widescreen option and playing a little game of 'which big lad can have the slittiest eyes in the picture.'

At the WACA with Monty and Freddie. Check out the one in the middle with the weird headgear and outsized face.

Sizing up the minature cricket ground outside the WACA;
trying to work out which player's Glenn McGrath,
so I can accidentally stand on him.

Adam Gilchrist just getting a little bit too carried away once
The Ashes are won, and getting himself to the top of
all England fans 'wanker lists' in the process.

It's Christmas time, there's no need to be afraid.
The Barmy Army BBQ gets drenched against a
backdrop of gloomy Melbourne.

The vast MCG on Boxing Day, a great Australian tradition.
Spot the join where the Great Southern Stand
meets the even greater new stand.

Like roasted lambs to the slaughter, England fans
queue patiently in Coogee's wilting heat to get tickets
for the fifth and final drubbing.

A church on George Street, Sydney. Final proof, not that it was
needed, that they take cricket pretty seriously round here.

WESTERN AUSTRALIA: THE WILDFLOWER STATE

10 December - Arrive Perth

So it was farewell to NZ. Maybe it's because we live in a tiny little country, but I just couldn't get my head round the changing time zones. I knew I had three planes to catch and that I left Auckland at seven in the morning and arrived in Perth mid-afternoon. How many hours had that taken? No idea and no major inclination to work it out either.

The day didn't start brilliantly with the news that Everton had lost 2-0 at Portsmouth. The bad tidings of both goals filtered through via texts as I was on the 15-minute shuttle bus ride to the airport. No big surprise there really; as soon as the advent calendars come out, the team always seems to bomb. Apparently James Beattie had an absolute 'mare as well. I take this personally as I publicly pronounced his transfer a 'hit' around 12 months ago.

The flights were spot on, as you would expect; the Australians have got the whole internal flying bit sussed. Good job really; you're not going to get far on your bike round here. Flying over the vast expanses, it was possible to make out some of the huge plumes of smoke, apparently coming from the latest series of bush fires. Victoria is the worst affected state and there is talk of some of the fires coming together to form a super-fire. This puts me in mind of the supergroups that came together in the 1970s. Hopefully the fires won't cause as much pain as they did.

If anything, there seems a lack of hysteria around the fires, but the authorities have developed methods of controlling them over the years. It seems incongruent that they are using loads of water to put out fires in Victoria, but there is a drought in Queensland; maybe that sort of thing comes with the massive territory. It makes me wonder if they've heard of Red Adair over here, the only famous fireman really, apart from Sam, Robbie off Grange Hill and the Pugh Twins and colleagues, who operated under the strict supervision of Trumpton's Captain Flack. Anyway it turns out that Red's dead, baby; dying of; yep you've guessed it, natural causes, at the grand old age of 89. Checking him out on the internet, there was a great quote saying 'I've done a deal with the devil. He said he's going to give me an air-conditioned place when I go down there, if I go there, so I won't put all the fires out."

One of my fellow passengers, who was returning home to Perth, had some pretty strong views on the Victorian Bush fires situation. Emphasising the parochialism and competitiveness of this country, he felt the Victorians have brought it on themselves. Apparently they could have done loads more 'back burning' to prevent this issue in advance. This is something the Western Australian authorities have had sussed for ages. Controversial stuff.

As I left New Zealand, the Test Series with Sri Lanka had really come to life as a result of some serious hullabaloo. This stemmed from an incident involving the run out of Muralitharan as he walked down the wicket to congratulate his Sri Lankan team-mate on a century. The bad feeling was apparently exacerbated because of a previous meeting between the two countries, when in a similar incident the Sri Lankans pardoned Kiwi Nathan Astle.

The New Zealanders remained indignant, saying it's 'sux of juan, and huf a dizzen of the ather' or words to that effect. Maybe dodgy levels of sportsmanship creep across the Tasman too.

Speaking of their near neighbours, it seems increasingly likely that Australia will select Andrew Symonds for the Perth Test. The TV people seem to make a point of prefixing Kevin Pietersen's name with a qualifying South African-born. I wonder if Symonds' English heritage will crop up quite as often?

England's cricket team had expectedly drawn their tour match against Western Australia, with some interesting individual displays. Strauss and Cook put on a monster opening partnership of 183 runs, apparently making batting look pretty straightforward. Hopefully they can carry on with this for the Third Test, a solid start would make a major difference to England. Next up, in an unaccustomed number three spot, Geraint Jones. He was out first ball and with Chris Read making 59, it was another decision for Fletcher and Flintoff to ponder. Having said that, the selection of Jones for the first two Tests wasn't based on weight of runs, so it probably won't make any difference.

If Cook and Strauss' partnership was impressive, there's another one in the offing to completely blow that away. Bindi Irwin, the unnervingly grown-up daughter of sadly deceased Steve, is planning a US Tour. And who's going to accompany her? You got it. Fresh from successfully integrating the new Yellow Wiggle, who's wearing the skivvy (as explained earlier) as if he was born in it, The Wiggles will be joining Miss Irwin in the good old US of A. Not since Peter Andre and Jordan got together has something just seemed so right.

Now, back in Adelaide did I mention something about hating a place upon arrival? Well Perth's rubbish.

Everyone from fellow plane passengers to the cab driver, was telling me what a beautiful place it was. Well my hotel is next to a building site, I can't get on the internet and the town seems largely deserted.

By the time I'd trudged down to an internet café it was starting to go dark, so I decided to head down to the Swan River. There were bound to be loads of places to eat and drink and unwind after spending an unspecified number of hours on a plane.

Nothing.

So I chose to lower my expectations and headed for a takeaway to grab something I could at least take back to the hotel and trough in my room. Nope - closed. I settled for a 7-11, thankfully there was a clue in the title so at least it was open. I grabbed myself a thoroughly makeshift tea, mainly consisting of crisps (because Tesco Express this wasn't) and traipsed back to the hotel, sulking.

Thought this place was meant to be good.

11 December

After having a word with myself, I decide to give Perth another chance. As it turned out, I'm in a decent spot, about half way between the City Centre and the WACA.

Braving the inevitable searing heat, I decided to wander down into town and guess what? It's alright is Perth. The people in the shops seemed genuinely friendly and asked 'How's your day?' with a sincerity at least bordering on genuine interest. The Aussie people away from the cricket have been generally polite and gracious to be honest, at least until you veer crazily onto the subject of sport. But these Western Australians were really nice.

This could stem from their strange yet seemingly proud boast that Perth is 'the most isolated city in the world'. When you are flying to Australia, at least to the east coast for Brisbane or Sydney, the most soul-destroying part is when you actually start flying over Oz itself. Three hours later (and you are still flying over Australia) is when the stir-craziness kicks in. In fact, Perth is closer to Indonesia than it is to Sydney. Go from London to Moscow, add on another 500 or so miles, and you've got the distance from Perth to Sydney.

The centre of Perth looked pretty smart really and in a pedestrianised area they had a couple of cricket nets set up and there were various events going on around the Test Match. Today there was the chance to meet Adam Hollioake and John Emburey. I managed to have a chat with Embers and it turned out he's pretty pleasant and affable. His language was also impeccable which was a bit of a shock as I remember reading in one of Simon Hughes' books that John once replied to an enquiry about his back injury with the immortal response 'The facking facker's facking facked'.

He felt that England could play two spinners at Perth. I took this as an opportunity to have a bit of a chuckle with him saying "Yeah, last time England won here they had two spinners, that Phil Edmonds, and I forget the name of the other fella." He accepted this in the spirit it was intended (almost a first on the tour) and we had a bit of a laugh. I then had a pic taken with Adam Hollioake too and figured this would be the end of my rubbing shoulders with ex-England Test players for the day. Little did I know.

After mooching back to the hotel (now the internet was working) I updated on Wiggles news, The *New York Times* has likened Greg Page's departure as similar to John Lennon or Paul McCartney leaving the Beatles. I couldn't help thinking that was way out of line and that such a famous publication should be ashamed.

John perhaps, but Paul was rubbish.

As the day meandered into evening, I made another attempt to get in touch with Sky Sports commentator David 'Bumble' Lloyd. This stems from the fact that he was also writing a blog for Yahoo and my contact there had said he would like to meet up with me in Oz. This seemed a bit far-fetched and after chatting to him in Adelaide, I got the impression that it wasn't going to happen.

My intention for the evening was to go out and grab something to eat and then head down to the designated Barmy Army pub, the delightfully named 'Lucky Shag'. This title is obviously a reference to the seabird the shag; subject of the Christopher Isherwood poem which begins with the line 'The common cormorant or shag, Lays eggs inside a paper bag'.

Anyway, I thought I'd ping Bumble a text on the off chance that he wanted to meet up. He did, tonight. Brilliant.

So I got sorted and got out there, a bit nervous like on a date or maybe a job interview or something, I needn't have worried, it was a top night.

Maybe this wasn't everybody's idea of meeting an amazing celebrity, but it had certain poignancy for me. My first cricket memories were predominantly TV based, watching the West Indies win everything and watching Lancashire on the box.

ITV's Roses coverage (did I mention I hate ITV?) was probably the most depressing live TV cricket coverage ever broadcast. The games were seemingly all played under slate grey skies, the cricket itself was turgid and if there was ever any chance of a positive result, the Leeds or Manchester rain would come along and scupper it. My vague recollection is that Martin Tyler and John Helm commentated. The camera work was pretty shoddy, the adverts arrived in the middle of overs and sometimes in the middle of (admittedly rare) exciting passages of play. Both counties were at a pretty low ebb; Yorkshire were rubbish, Lancs probably slightly worse. Lancs batsman David 'Bumble' Lloyd was a central figure in this, and also captained the county in the mid-70s.

I arranged to meet the great man in this pretty swish bar, away from the city centre, and I was pleased to note that he already had a pint when I walked in. He clocked me straight away and once I'd got my pint we shook hands and away we went.

The evening kicked off with a mutual bemoaning of the technical difficulties we were having in doing the blog, although I suspect he had a serious advantage on me from Sky Sports' commentary position.

What was great about meeting him was that he immediately put me at ease and we just started chatting about sport like most blokes would when they meet up for the first time. In fact, it was fair to say that just about every former cricketer I had met had been genial and patient, and made me speculate on whether this would be the case if it was ex-footballers I was dealing with. Not a sniff I guess.

Naturally, conversation turned to the disaster of Adelaide and Bumble was forthright in his views. He felt that England had completely frozen on the day and taken on a wholly negative approach. His view was that if England expected to block Warne all day, they got exactly what was coming to them. Of course he was right. Despite his 40 wickets in England last year, the batsmen were aggressive which meant that his long spells were going for a few runs as well.

Bumble really thought that England lacked aggression and by picking a team to draw, they got what they deserved.

A bottle of white then appeared and the conversation and wine flowed nicely. It was interesting to hear that he felt a lot of England's problems actually stemmed from Flintoff's injury. The knock-on effect of this was playing an extra bowler, so batting Freddie at number six. "He's not a number six," said Bumble, "He's a seven, a Gilchrist." It was hard to argue with this logic. This also had the domino effect on England's famous tail, hardly bolstered by Ashley Giles' presence.

The conversation broadened to talk about football; he's a big fan, especially of Accrington Stanley (his home town) and Macclesfield (near where he lives now) and knows Robbie Savage pretty well. His views on Lancashire County Cricket club were very interesting to me, but tour rules apply there.

Also from what I gleaned from the evening, suffice to say, I don't think I'll be trying to get a night out with Ian Botham in the near future, not sure I could take the pace, though I'm pretty sure Beefy won't let this news get him down too much.

Bumble is also a music lover and rattled off his favourites in a way reminiscent of David Brent in *The Office*. Brent said "Cleese, Everett, Milligan.........Sessions." and then stared creepily at the camera. Mr Lloyd said "Stones, Dylan, Springsteen" and was pretty indignant when I suggested that surely it was time for the Stones to turn it in.

As I was unaware of whether the night would just consist of a quick pint and then him scooting off, I felt privileged to have a proper drink and chat with him. A genuinely lovely fella. So after we'd eaten it was a case of HIM asking ME what I was doing next. It had to be the aforementioned Lucky Shag, but I didn't know where it was. Observing Bumble, with his classic East Lancs brogue, asking an unsuspecting waitress, whether she knew the exact whereabouts of the pub, was worth the cost of the entire trip alone.

"Hello Love. Now I'm a pommie, and this is going to sound like a funny question, but, can you tell me where we might find the Lucky Shag?"

What made it better was she was new there and didn't have a clue.

Anyway we found the Shag, and it turned out to be a brilliant boozer, with a major outdoor drinking area, right on the edge of the Swan River, perfect. As we waited for a cab, Bumble decided he was going to lay some cricket trivia questions on me, and this proved to be a source of some frustration, especially with his dead-pan ability to let me know I was wrong, but wind me up a little.

Example; my answer, Damien Fleming.

Bumble: "Damien Fleming you say (he's now nodding vigorously), Victorian, Right Arm, Seamer (he's smiling with the look of someone who's genuinely pleased you've got the answer right), it's not 'im!!". Yeah, cheers mate.

It was quite funny for me to walk into the Lucky Shag with Bumble as people I didn't know actually spoke to me by association. Loads of them wanted their pic taken with him and it was all really funny. I was a bit bevvied by now, and was pleased to drink another few Coopers with him.

He sloped off before the end of the night, and I was honestly thrilled to have met him. Great.

Think I quite like Perth now.

12 December

Having woken up with the inevitable hangover I decided it was time to do some exercise. Don't get me wrong, it's not like I'm Daley Thompson when at home, but the constant eating and boozing was taking its toll.

My choice was to hire a bike and after we had gone through the customary preliminary of "Are you here for the cricket?" chat, I was off around a six or seven-mile circuit that takes you right around the city along the banks of the Swan River. It's a really neat place and like all Aussie cities, cycle paths are supplied to make it nice and easy to get around.

This kind of gave an insight into the Aussie sporting prowess. The climate makes such a big difference and on my travels I saw walkers, joggers, cyclists and rollerbladers. By contrasting this with driving to a gloomy 'health club' in the rain back home, you started to see the reality.

I also felt slightly inadequate cycling around at a relatively gentle pace (although I still had a proper sweat on) in my T-shirt and shorts ensemble, as a lot of the locals had got all the lycra gear on and were going at a searing pace. It wouldn't have surprised me to get sledged by one of the Aussie blokes as he sped past me, something like "Ave a go ya mug" or maybe "Get back to the velo-drome, dickhead." Next time I'll definitely ask for a bike without a basket on the front.

When I got over the other side of the river I was in the slightly less affluent part of Perth. Some of the riverside apartments there appeared to have only three bedrooms rather than the ones with several more. Slumming it or what? Anyway, the exercise did me good.

The plan for the evening was to make a first trip down to the WACA and watch a Twenty20 legends game between England and Australia, featuring my old mate John Emburey amongst others. I had already picked up a ticket, as a crowd of around 15,000 was expected, not bad for a charity game.

The WACA proved to be very similar in layout to the Adelaide Oval. Two big grass banks, this time situated square of the wicket, and decent sized stands at each side. It was still a pleasant cricket oval, but in comparison to the pristine ground in Adelaide, was starting to look a bit dated really. There had been talk that this year's Ashes Test could possibly be the last, with a brand new development containing a huge new cricket stadium replacing the WACA. Having said all that, the facilities at the WACA, and in partic-ular the impressive floodlights, would put almost all English grounds to shame.

Being able to meander down to the ground in the early evening sunshine and then settle down on the grass bank and relax was a pleasure really, and it was also cathartic to be watching a game that wasn't exactly critical. Having said that, I'm sure all the

England fans there joined me in being really keen to see England win, you know, just to see how it felt.

As tends to happen in these games, the youngest players came to the fore and Western Australian Ryan Campbell, who only retired at the end of last season, helped the Aussies rack up a decent total of 170.

One of the best moments of the evening was the appearance of Billy Cooper, the Barmy Army Trumpeter, on the field of play in the interval. I'd met Billy a couple of times and he was a nice dude; a very inconspicuous sort who was definitely good at what he did. He played alongside an Aussie trumpeter and this was well received, especially among the England supporters in what turned out to be a hugely impressive 17,000 strong crowd. It was also confirmed now that Billy would be allowed in the ground for the Test Match. Good sense prevailing at last.

The England legends started their reply disastrously with Mike Gatting out first ball, but later Graham Thorpe and Robin Smith appeared to be guiding England home comfortably. Then, surprise surprise, a clatter of quick wickets and we were up against it. The end game scenario was England needing 19 to win off the last two overs with former Surrey team-mates Alec Stewart and Adam Hollioake at the wicket.

Australia then took the bizarre decision to bring on former wicket keeper and current Channel Nine commentator Ian Healy on to bowl. Hollioake thought it was Christmas and helped himself with the over going like this

6......6......1......1......2......6

Job done, and an England win witnessed on tour, nice one.

It hadn't been a brilliant few days for Healy, who'd mistakenly stated on air that Matthew Hayden had a pink handle on his bat in support of Breast Research. Good work if you can get it. That'll be Breast Cancer Research, Ian.

After the game it was back to the Lucky Shag. I'd had an idea that I could get an interview with Billy the Trumpeter and then send it in to Radio Five Live. He was more than happy to help and we sat down in the pub and nailed it first time in a couple of minutes. I was pretty proud of my opening question 'Billy, you've been described as the most controversial Ashes figure since Douglas Jardine, how does that feel?' Hopefully they would broadcast the interview at some stage.

So a successful evening all round really, and only one more day and then the vital third Test Match would be upon us.

13 December

It is sad to report that the locals here are operating under some kind of delusion and I really don't know how to shatter their world. You see even though the temperature is operating in the 90s today, they seem to be labouring under the misapprehension that it'll be Christmas soon. All the shops are kitted out and there are school kids in the street singing carols and that. The problem is that it's so hot that the artificial snow on the decorations is on the verge of melting. Surely Yuletide here must take place towards the end of June or something.

The other problem with the whole 'Christmas in summer' thing is singing songs about snow and sleighs. Doesn't really check out, and it seems almost certain that many of the kids here have only ever seen snow on TV anyway. Some of the carols actually have the words changed to make it more fitting for the Aussie climate, and they also needed to turn to a famous Australian songsmith to come up with a legit carol. There was only one choice; Ladies and Gentlemen, Mr Rolf Harris. Here are the lyrics to one of his carols;

Western Australia: The Wildflower State

Early on one Christmas Day, a Joey Kanga-roo,
Was far from home and lost in a great big zoo.
Mummy, where's my mummy, they've taken her a-way,
We'll help you find your mummy son, hop on the sleigh.

Chorus:
Six white boomers, snow white boomers,
Racing Santa Claus through the blazing sun.
Six white boomers, snow white boomers,
On his Aus-tra-lian run

So the premise here is that when he visits Oz, six big white kangaroos propel Santa's sleigh forward. There are no details on whether one of them has a very shiny nose. Other Australian carols include, *Let Us Barbeque, Deck the sheds with bits of wattle* and the brilliant *Wayne wants a surfboard for Christmas.* Seriously, these songs do exist.

My previous Australia trip included Christmas Day in a place called Wagga Wagga, the locals just call it Wagga, which is a small town which once supplied the opening partnership for Australia, in the shape of Michael Slater and Mark Taylor. Sitting outside drinking ice-cold lager in the 100-degree shade eating crisps and bits of sausage and that, certainly has its charms, but it just doesn't really feel like Christmas.

Continuing the festive theme, I was watching the Australian equivalent of the old *Richard and Judy Show* (should that be Pinch and Judy show?) This Morning, honestly there was nothing else on, and they were talking about Chris Cringle, apparently the Aussie version of Secret Santa. A viewer had e-mailed in to explain that he had picked somebody out in his works Secret Santa that he didn't like.So he decided to spend the money on "a $5 bet on the Poms to win the Ashes because this was never going to happen." This was followed by a seemingly endless period of guffawing around the studio. Ooh my aching sides.

On the other hand, there is a TV show in Australia called *The Back Page* where they discuss all sporting matters, which, now they are starting to get over Ian Thorpe's un-Australian action, is pretty much a cricket show. I was tuned into a debate about the Barmy Army.

What I saw was absolutely amazing. The deference and respect for the Barmy Army is staggering. The fact that England can muster up a group of fans following them around the world is undoubtedly impressive, especially as the Army was spawned in a period when England cricket success was so minimal. The Barmy tag was actually added by the Aussie media, who couldn't understand why such a poor team would have significant support. This probably says a great deal about Australia, (good and bad) and a lot about England too.

Anyway the mad thing was the quote from the panel on the show when debating the spoilsport tactics of the 'fun police' and in particular the banning of Billy the Trumpeter. They said: "The Barmy Army is the single greatest thing ever to happen to Test cricket." Amazing. Having met quite a few people connected with the BA during this trip, I reckon this would almost embarrass them. And all the Aussies on the show were in total unison about how brilliant the Barmy Army is. Giving credit to the opposition for anything seemed really out of character, to be 'bigging' them up to this extent, was just eerie.

On the Barmy front, I had received a text from home to say that the Billy interview had been trailed on air and was due to go out in about 20 minutes. This gave me a real sense of pride. Half an hour later this was scuppered as my thunder had been stolen by none other than the Ipswich Ripper, as a press conference on this subject had been hastily called, and therefore broadcast instead of my interview. Not fair. There are loads of people with loads bigger reasons to say this than me, but I hope they lock him up and throw away the key.

14 December – Day 1 Perth Test
Australia 244
England 51-2

What a day!

Things started with a leisurely stroll to the WACA and a reversal of the news from Day One in Adelaide, no we hadn't won the toss and yes, at last, praise be, Monty was in the side. He had come in for Giles and in another change Saj Mahmood was in for Jimmy Anderson. You know, by the Fifth Test in Sydney we may actually pick our best team. That'd be nice.

The Monty information was definitely tempered by the news about the Aussies electing to bat first on what was thought to be a pretty benign surface. The major fear was that Australia would pile up a massive total á la Brisbane, and then England would face batting for three days to save the Ashes. Little did we know.

My ticket was for one of the grass bank areas, but I was disappointed to note that the Barmy Army tourists were situated in the seating area, so no real chance of a re-creation of the excellent set up at Adelaide, never mind. My next goal was to find some shade, because once again, it was hot. The amount of shade was minimal in the entire ground, obviously the Aussies can handle it better, but it seemed odd for a country that places a huge emphasis on its 'SunSmart' campaign. Cancer of the skin is the most common form in Australia, so you would think more would be done. In fairness, there was a free sun tan lotion dispenser, although a decent queue was forming.

Luckily, I had stumbled across a kind of gazebo thingy, which had actually been put in place to shelter some members/corporate sections, but also hung over onto a walkway. It meant standing up, but I had a spot in the shade, and unsurprisingly mostly Englishmen occupied this area. Some definitely fitted into the Uber-Pom category, but never mind, shade was good.

As you would expect, the Aussies started confidently and as always, aggressively. You have to hand it to Langer and Hayden, they are not going to die wondering and, despite the fact that they sometimes ride their luck, a fast start can dictate terms for the rest of the day, innings or even match. So 40 plus on the board after 10, and it looked for all the world that it was a long, hot day in the field for England. Then Hoggy got Hayden out and this brought key-man Ponting to the wicket, who along with Langer saw them through to drinks. I took this opportunity to get myself a drink, and after queuing for a bit and returning to my spot I heard a massive cheer. Giving it legs up the steps to get to see what had happened, I discovered that Harmison had snared Ponting. Wow, it was all starting to look a little different.

England kept things really quiet for a spell and then came what everyone had been waiting for, Monty-time. To be honest, we'd be waiting about three weeks too long for it, but here it was, no need to worry about that right now.

It was a pretty bold and aggressive move by Freddie, treating Monty in the same way as the Aussies treat Warne really, an attacking bowler, there to take wickets, not to contain while the main bowlers had a breather. Monty looked pretty confident as he strode up for his first delivery, and he was spot on from the start, In fact, his first over was flawless, a maiden, and the Aussies seemed to be showing him some respect. There is no doubt that they know he's a better bowler than Gilo, and it was obvious they would be looking to get after him at some stage.

Four minutes later, Monty started his second over and then it happened. Buoyed by his first six deliveries, there was a sense of expectancy as he came up to bowl. You sort of knew something had to give; the Aussies wouldn't block him all day. Then Langer came forward to defend once again, and the sight of the bails coming off was a joy to behold. The English fans in the crowd went absolutely crazy, but this paled into insignificance compared to Monty. He ran around the loop, whooping and beaming as he went, generally missing high fives with his team-mates. The best way to describe his joy when he takes a wicket is unbridled. In fact, 'the Monty' goes a little like this.

1. A look of utter disbelief
2. Give yourself a little clap
3. Go skipping round the pitch like Michael Flatley on acid
4. Miss loads of high fives
5. Calm down a few minutes later

So that was lunch and the Aussies were three wickets down with a paltry, by their standards, 69 runs on the board. Dreamland for England really.

I went to grab a celebratory beer and meet up with Chris, a Blackpool fella I knew, and was accosted by a lad who recognised me from Everton, so we had a proper chat about all things blue. Maybe the fans of the 'so-called' big clubs spent all their money on Champions League away trips, but it seemed like half of Goodison was over in Australia.

After having a couple of lunchtime drinks it was back to my shaded spot. This was at the opposite end of the ground from the Barmy Army, but quite simply there were no spare seats on Day One and shade seemed like a priority in any case. Even from this vantage point, it was obvious that Billy was in fine form with his trumpet, running through the full repertoire. It was interesting that not that many English people knew the words to *Jerusalem*, but everyone could join together in unison to sing "I shagged Matilda, I shagged Matilda and so did my mates" to the tune of Australia's traditional anthem. To any Australians reading (congratulations), yes, we all do know Matilda is a sheep.

England's priority after lunch was to get more wickets and they came out with a real spring in their step. Monty was still purposeful, but the other bonus was that Steve Harmison started to look more like his old self. Steaming in with real aggression he was making the Aussie batsmen really hop around and then took a brilliant caught and bowled to get rid of Clarke.

This brought the English-born Andrew Symonds to the crease. His one-day record was excellent, but there were definite question marks around his Test career. All those in the shaded area, at least 50% of whom were Man City fans, agreed that if we could get Symonds early, we were well on the way. So this seemed like a vital moment in the day's play.

Symonds seemed pretty edgy as he survived a couple of appeals and then a seriously close run out chance. This seemed to change his attitude and, as Monty appeared to be tiring, he'd bowled 12 overs unchanged, the Sideshow Bob-haired English Aussie decided that Panesar had to go. He took 17 off five Monty deliveries, including two towering sixes.

This was a serious test for Monty now. The Aussie supporters, who had been surprised by their side's stuttering start, were at last making some noise. They are good at making noise. Their reaction to joyous events has much more of an American feel to it, loads of whooping and hollering, with quite a few high-fives thrown in for good measure. Honestly, you wouldn't realise they were part of our Empire at times, which makes it all the more important to remind them - regularly.

Monty and the England fans had the last laugh. In his 14th over, he snared Symonds with a classic edge to the keeper, the error-prone Geraint Jones grabbed it at the second attempt, and it's time for 'the Monty' again, the run, the leap, the joy and once again just missing the hands of his teammates. In his next over it got even better as danger man Gilchrist fell under the wizardry of the newly named 'Sikh of Tweak' and the Aussies were in trouble.

At tea they were six down and now things started to cool down a bit so it was time for me to go and join the Barmies to sample a bit of the atmosphere at the other end of the ground. The mood was euphoric and everybody seemed so chuffed that Monty has prospered. The Americans talk about 'Monday morning quarterbacks,' those who are wise after the sporting event. Not the case here. Everybody wanted Monty in the side from day one and now it felt like 'our selection' choice had been completed vindicated.

The Barmy Army were in great voice, regularly regaling the Australian fans with *God Save YOUR Gracious Queen*. The response from the Australians was largely unintelligible, but a new song they had developed seemed to end with 'Piss Off Home.' It was necessary to point out to them that we were 'home' really, and that they should think of their country as a holiday retreat for English people, a sort of England-on-Sea maybe.

Back on the pitch and Monty's day just got better and better, and he led the England team off mid-way through the final session, having taken five wickets and bowled 24 overs unchanged from his first ball in his Ashes career. Brilliant. The reception he received from the England fans was amazing, but in fairness the whole ground rose to his efforts. The fact that Harmison had taken four wickets was significant too, and it just made you wonder, if they could keep firing, maybe England had a chance in this series after all.

Now England needed a good hour and guess what? The opening partnership got into the 30s and then perished. Again. Alastair

Cook's dismissal was quickly followed by Bell and the day probably ended pretty even.

For me, another highlight was yet to come. My Radio Five Live efforts were supposed to end in Adelaide but the lad who was covering Perth had been delayed so I had been given the nod to operate as Fans' Reporter for a couple more days. What's more, because of the change in time zones, Perth is only eight hours ahead of the UK, the chat would take place from the commentary box.

So a few minutes before the end of play, I blagged my way into the Bradman Suite and stood outside awaiting my call, feeling pretty nervous again. I felt like a bit of a cricket groupie hanging around outside and probably looked to others like the oldest auto-graph hunter in the world. My only company outside was indeed a young English lad who had snuck in to try to get some famous sig-natures, but he was loads more composed than me.

As soon as play finished and Atherton, Martin-Jenkins and many others streamed out, I steamed in. I was swiftly plonked in the Five Live commentary position, next to Alec Stewart, who shook my hand and wished me luck. The format was for Matthew Bannister to chat with Alec and then to play some of the stuff I'd recorded during the day. It was wholly unnerving to hear this played back through my headphones and I remarked to the BBC producer lady next to me that I sounded drunk, which I thought I did a bit. She looked slightly alarmed and asked if I was, and I quickly reas-sured her that I was fine. It was a good job really, we were on the air in a few seconds and my replacement was still on his way round the world.

Then Matthew spoke to me and its hard to recall exactly what I said, but it seemed to go OK, as we talked about the two people whose presence and talent had made this one of the best days of the tour, Monty and Billy.

And then I took my 'cans' off (getting the broadcasting lingo off pat now) and disappeared from the scene. Definitely two of my fifteen minutes of fame, and a proper buzz to be honest.

As I strode from the ground I could see a copy of the local morning newspaper on the floor. It was running an Ashes Special. The headline? 'Our Warriors poised to finish off the Poms.'

We were far from finished, we had Monty.

15 December – Day 2 Perth Test
Australia 244 & 119-1
England 219

Strolling down to the WACA today, there was a real feeling of optimism. A wholly unrealistic hypothetical scenario is often played out in sport along the lines of would you have accepted that score-line at the start of play? England's response would have had to be a resounding YES. Losing two wickets was a blow, but we'd had a good day, no two ways about it. What was required next was for England to have a good opening session, and then we could be looking at ramming home the advantage. A series score line of 2-1 with two to play was a mouth-watering prospect.

But that's getting ahead of ourselves, England had to capitalise on their good work of yesterday. They failed to do that but it was another spellbinding day of cricket.

First things first, the weather. It was properly hot today, steamy you might say, and a place in the shade was the only thing to do. I was a bit on the late side and it was pretty chocka in there, luckily there was a spirit of camaraderie and my fellow sheltering Englishmen (and women) soon made room for me in our makeshift sanctuary. I noticed one or two Aussies had made their way in there, it seemed fair to point out to them that this was the away end and that they should be used to the heat, luckily they saw the funny side. To be frank, we were all just hugely grateful to be under there.

From our vantage point it was hard to say whether Australia bowled brilliantly or not, but England's batsmen appeared to have resorted to Adelaide mode, failing to score off the first two overs. Then one of the players who could hold his head up really high after Adelaide, Paul Collingwood, was caught behind and the bad vibes started again. Australia had certainly posted a sub-par first innings, England were in grave danger of failing to get past it. By drinks, they had added a measly 36 more runs and lost Strauss to boot, perhaps another dodgy decision, so were four wickets down.

It was time to clutch at straws now and hope that Freddie would rediscover his batting form. He'd been badly out of sorts but the potentially explosive partnership with Pietersen looked like England's last chance of getting up to Australia's total. The crowd were pretty quiet at this stage, everyone knowing that this was a critical passage of play. Pietersen and Flintoff both looked pretty positive, if they could have got through to lunch together, England may still have been on level terms in the game.

That was a big 'if'. As the wise man once said 'If my Auntie had bollocks she would have been my Uncle', and so it proved. If Geraint Jones is the king of the costly error, challenged by Gilo the King of Spain in Adelaide, Freddie is undoubtedly the Clown Prince of 'getting out to the opposition's worst bowler.' In fairness to Freddie and Andrew Symonds, the Birmingham-born Australian adoptee is a no mug.

The decision to bring Symonds on ahead of Warne was a shock, especially after Monty's success yesterday. Shocking maybe but inspired, definitely. Symonds cleaned up Freddie and Jones and England were in deep, deep trouble. They'd blown it again. Were the Aussies that good, or were we just spineless? You had to say it looked like men against boys really, with the 2005

Ashes vintage stature of Marcus Trescothick, Simon Jones and Michael Vaughan replaced by the more brittle Cook, Mahmood and Collingwood.

Lunch came and went all too quickly, just like Saj Mahmood's innings and England were still more than a hundred behind. The Aussie lady stood next to me was starting to get on my nerves a bit by pointing out every minute just exactly how many runs England were behind. 'I'm guessing you're a statistician or a Maths teacher round here with skills like that are you?' I suggested. As it turned out, she was a teacher! After my initial embarrassment was out of the way I had a good natter with her and her son, both of whom turned out to be really sound.

After seeing England's next wicket fall, I decided to brave the conditions and make a move. This was partly because I wanted to get into the atmosphere with the Barmies, but also because I wanted to record the reaction to Monty coming out to bat for the radio. For once my timing was impeccable.

The Barmy Army were starting to hit full voice and 'You all live in a Convict colony' (to the tune of Yellow Submarine) was being sung with gusto, complimented by Billy's trumpeting. The Fanatics reply was impressive, by their own hideously low standards, a song about Ricky Ponting being magic, and wearing the baggy cap. The familiar tune was meant to be *My Old Man's A Dustman*, but because it was Aussies singing everybody just shrieked their own tune, with every note sounding like a dying breath.

God forbid but if there is an Aussie X-factor the TV studios will be surrounded by packs of dogs and there will be broken windows for a 50-mile radius, which could do some serious collateral damage around here. I can see the newspaper headlines now 'Four houses damaged in singing incident.'

On the pitch KP was really chancing his arm and once Hoggard went, he threw caution to the wind. Then came one of the highlights of the tour so far. Pietersen skied one into the deep and you could see it was going to fall just inside the boundary.

Question for any England fan: If one of the Aussie fielders was going to drop a catch, who would you want it to be?

Answer: Maybe Ponting, Warne, Symonds...no wait a minute......definitely Glenn McGrath.

Question: Would you have any preference whereabouts on the field of play it happened?

Answer: Don't mind as long as it's near the England fans.

You'll never guess what happened next. Yep, Glenn spilled the chance and the England support went apeshit. And the ball went for four. And, just to add to the indignity of the moment, a couple of balls later McGrath was moved to a different fielding position. The cheers had hardly died down and then had to start again.

Flight to Australia 700 quid, Beer money, too much to calculate, Seeing Glenn McGrath drop a catch in front of the Barmy Army, priceless.

Pietersen added a six and a four for good measure, but was out soon afterwards, for a useful 70. Now it was Monty time.

As the England support sang his name, you could see Monty's brilliant smile beaming away. He was enjoying himself, and why ever not? The Pietersen innings and the dropped catch had meant that a bit of momentum had shifted to England, but they were still a critical 69 runs behind, I'd worked that out without the aid of one of Australia's leading minds.

Rapturous applause greeted Monty's first act with the bat, digging out a 94mph yorker from Brett Lee. We had ourselves a new hero. If only Sports Personality of the Year was decided in January. No, scratch that, if only they'd have picked him when they should have done.

Then something wonderful happened. Harmison and Panesar looked as though the weight and pressure of the situation had been lifted from them and they played with a real sense of freedom. Monty hit three boundaries, the first two off Warne, and they were greeted with resounding cheers. The last, off Stuart Clarke, was initially greeted with an awed sense of hush. The straight drive is a pure cricket shot. The perfect execution of this shot is one of the great sights to behold. To see this affected by Monty, our hero, was a surreal and beautiful moment. And after the initial momentary silence, everyone went mental, obviously.

Finally, Clark got Harmison out, Monty finished on 16 not out, not bad for someone who supposedly couldn't be risked because of his batting, and the last wicket partnership had added 40 potential priceless runs. This was also the highest partnership of the innings, amazing really.

Sadly, brilliant though it was, that was as good as it got. Hoggard's first ball dismissal of Langer was a false dawn, as the Aussie Juggernaut relentlessly progressed and Hayden and Ponting assembled the first century partnership of the game. The day deteriorated as the fun police also started throwing their weight around in the Barmy section as well. It's really hard to take coppers seriously when they are wearing shorts, but they were pretty severe, ejecting people when it really didn't seem necessary. I kept well out of the way on account of my arrestable face.

There was a nice moment towards the end of the day which evoked memories of watching cricket from Australia as a kid, seeing the birds scatter as the ball or a toiling fielder approached The sun was starting to give us a break and a large number of seagulls had assembled on the outfield. The match situation, England's bowlers and the crowd were all thoroughly becalmed at this stage. Nothing much was happening out there. Then the fans were roused to life by the fact that Matthew Hayden had reached his half-century, and the applause reverberated around the ground. This prompted the squadron of gulls into action, and as they flew gracefully, against an azure blue sky, they encircled the ground. It seemed like their own Red Arrows style fly past, to salute the Aussie batsmen's achievement. Good that.

After that it was a quick trot up to the Five Live commentary box, where Alec Stewart suggested England 'need a miracle' to avoid defeat in the game. I managed to slag Aussies off a bit in my slot, saying that their fans would already have gone home if they were in England's position, and vowing that I'd be following England all the way to the, potentially bitter, end.

So that was the end of my broadcasting for now, most enjoyable. As I was departing the scene, the genial Alec Stewart asked me 'Where are you and the lads heading tonight?'

'Lucky Shag' I replied, quick as a flash. It was the single most quizzical look I've ever had from a former England cricket captain.

16 December – Day 3 Perth Test
Australia 244 & 527-5 declared
England 219 and 19-1

The Shag was fine again last night, but there was maybe a feeling that England's tenuous hold on the Ashes was coming to a close.

Still, you've got to go and have a look haven't you? I made my way down to the WACA with Chris and noticed something immediately. Today it was stupidly hot.

Luckily we made it in plenty of time and he took his seat as I made my way under the makeshift veranda for the third consecutive day. If ever England needed early wickets this was the day. It was definitely possible to win a cricket game scoring the highest total in the fourth innings, but it is pretty unusual. The other thing to be aware of was this game was well advanced, 21 wickets in two days, so a result was inevitable, a draw was not an option.

Western Australia: The Wildflower State

So England needed to find a way of achieving the miracle demanded by Alec Stewart. An Aussie collapse was the order of the day. And we kind of got that really.

Sadly, especially for those concerned, this was due to the high temperature and referred to those in the crowd, the First Aid tents were stuffed out as the oppressive heat took its toll. I loved my shady spot, and despite that we were all dripping with sweat under there, it was a lifesaver. It still seems amazing that there is so little shade at the WACA.

On the pitch, England were seriously up against it. I had bemoaned the use of Pietersen as a bowler when we really needed wickets in Adelaide, and inexplicably KP bowled two of the first three overs of the day, at a cost of 20 runs. The Aussies really must have believed it genuinely was Christmas. They were not prepared to pass up these gifts. Same old England really, no plan, devoid of ideas when the pressure was really on. This was painful to watch, yet again we had been in a winning position in the game, and it was all turning to nothing.

England did pick up two wickets in the morning session, but already they were more than 200 behind and the writing was appearing on the wall. Billy the Trumpeter resorted to playing the plaintive *Little Donkey*, continuing to impress with his range of tunes, but this sombre refrain matched the mood of the England support. It was hard to get behind a team who were being so comprehensively outplayed.

In the afternoon session Australia's relentless progress continued. The highlight for all the England fans in the ground was the appearance of the Freemantle Doctor. Having heard about and been bamboozled by this as a kid, I finally got to experience this phenomenon. For those who don't know, this is the name of the cooling afternoon sea breeze that comes blowing in to Perth down the coast from Freemantle, cooling everyone in its wake. The good

Doc puts his hardest work in during December and January, when the temperature differential between the land and ocean is greatest. The relief was palpable and we finally had some let-up in the heat. In the good old days of pacey, bouncy Perth wickets, the Doctor used to assist the fastest bowlers' velocity to exaggerate to speed at which they were bowling. You kind of figured now that even if England had the Freemantle Hurricane at their backs, the Aussies would still easily repel them.

There was a nice moment for the locals when Western Australian Mike Hussey reached his century. You've really got to hand it to Hussey, his record in this series has been exemplary, and his partnerships, especially with that pesky Ricky Ponting, totally critical. He is dogged with the bat, tenacious and brilliant in the field, and seems to have that mentality which singles out winners. He was given his chance to get in the Test side relatively late in his career, and has grabbed it with both hands. The nickname of Mr Cricket is not misplaced.

Tea came and went and it was clear that the Australians were in complete control of the game. They had their foot on England's throat; all that remained to see was how hard they wanted to press on. Michael 'Bowling Machine' Clarke eased his way to another century, but this seemed pretty irrelevant. What followed was an epic onslaught of almost biblical proportions. We were up against it, no doubt, so the last thing we needed was for the most destructive batsman in World cricket to do the business.

Adam Gilchrist is one of those players, if you don't get him out pretty early; he's going to score loads of runs really quickly. He zoomed to his half-century in just 40 balls, playing some crashing drives off all the bowlers England could serve up, and this represented his fastest ever Test 50. The game situation was curious really, the Aussies almost had enough runs to defend, but England would have had over two days to bat. So, if they batted for most of that time, they would win. It was strange; someone had to make some sense of it.

Step forward Adam Gilchrist. Once he reached his 50, he went absolutely bonkers. He made a whirling dervish seem completely becalmed and restrained. Monty was the first to feel the heat. His next four balls went SIX, SIX, FOUR and SIX. Each time you saw the ball go in the air you prayed for it to go in the general direction of a fielder. In most cases it did, the problem was the ball was about 100 feet in the air as it passed the powerless Englishman. You had to feel for Monty, having enjoyed a dream first day, this was turning into a total nightmare.

Mercifully Clarke saw off the next over, but his batting was just a sideshow really, the support act to the main performer. Monty gamely stepped up to bowl the next over, but Freddie was having none of it, passing the ball to the redoubtable Hoggard. Just to make things worse Clarke got involved, hitting consecutive fours before a single brought Gilchrist back onto strike. All of England's fielders were on the boundary, Freddie must have seriously contemplated putting Jones back as well. Next ball, a mighty hook for six more. The ground was totally buzzing. English, Aussie or other, everyone in attendance was aware we were seeing something amazing. You had to laugh and marvel at it really. As is the way at Test matches these days, loads of people had those 'over the ear' radios you can buy, so many were tuned into the Australian broadcast. The buzz around the ground was that Gilchrist could be on course to score the fastest hundred in Test history. The record is a hundred off 56 balls by Viv Richards. Despite having taken 40 balls for his first fifty, amazingly there was still a chance.

Steve Harmison must have been thinking 'thanks a bunch, pal' as his mate Freddie tossed him the ball. It seems like an extraordinarily stupid thing to say, but Harmy did quite well, restricting Gilchrist to no sixes and a paltry 15 runs off the over.

So at the start of Hoggard's over, he'd got 96 off 53, so 45 off the last 13 balls. Amazing. He needed a boundary to break the record and send everyone into total delirium. It was hard to know what to think really, it felt churlish to not want him to break the record.

That was a total lie by the way. Sour grapes or not, the tiniest, crumbiest little crumb of comfort, there was no way I wanted him to do it. Hoggy restricted him to a single, and then off the potentially record-breaking ball, intelligently bowled him a wide one, not quite wide enough to be called 'wide', and the chance had gone.

Well bowled Hoggy. Killjoy, wet blanket, spoilsport, whatever, all the Englishmen who had seen the first three Tests had seen enough Aussie euphoria to last a lifetime, even this, the hollowest of hollow victories, was something. When he quickly reached his hundred off 57 balls, everybody stood and acclaimed this masterful innings. It was brutal and exhausting to watch, but you had to admire it, albeit through gritted teeth.

Shell-shocked, I decided to wander over to the Barmy section, maybe to oversee the last rites of England's Ashes chances. The Aussies had declared and to make things worse, Strauss was out in the first over. Another dodgy decision by the look of things, he must have killed an umpire in a previous life.

The England fans, resigning themselves to another Aussie victory, decided that they may as well sing their way to defeat. To the tune of *Walking in a Winter Wonderland*, the song went a little like this:

There's only one Glenn McGrath
One Glenn McGrath
With his pension book and his zimmerframe
Glenn McGrath has pissed himself again

Western Australia: The Wildflower State

Even the usually surly Aussie sledge king was having a bit of a chuckle to that one.

The Aussie fans were happily making their way past, goading anyone they could recognise as English (basically those without the shit stars on their flags) as they made their way home, presumably for the eight day journey back to a Western Australian outpost. One bloke decided he'd speak to me

Aussie: We've decided it's not Gilchrist, but G – I – L – Christ
Me: I've been here four weeks mate and that's the single cleverest thing an Aussie has said to me, and its still shite.

This sounded spiteful, but he caught me on a bad day.

I met up with my mate Chris, who'd bailed earlier in the day due to the heat and his seat in the sun. He was delighted not to have seen the Gilchrist innings. A veteran of several Ashes tours, he has built a healthy dislike for Australians. The problem he has is that he feels duty bound to go back every time just in case that series is 'the one'. We decided to go for something to eat and ended up in the same gaff as I'd visited with Bumble.

It was rammed, not a shock on a Saturday night so we ended up virtually sharing a table with a couple. He was a proper chatty geezer, the sort who would ask you your name in the first minute of conversation. He then moved onto cricket, but this was pretty tame stuff, nothing too troubling. He was with his bird so there was no need to bite. Anyway, he needed a cig so went outside and his girlfriend leaned over to whisper something to me, and I had no idea what she was going to blurt out. She said "I'm the happiest girl in the world, that guy there has just asked me to move in with him and you're the first person I've told.' Resisting the temptation to say 'It'll never last love,' I instead proffered my congratulations. A nice moment.

She thought she was feeling lucky, and so were we, off to the casino.

The place was absolutely massive. The Aussies gamble around six times more per head than we do, and now it was easy to see why. Part of me wondered whether super casinos were a good idea for the UK, especially as there were loads of bevvied kids around too. Looking at this place I still figured it would be positive for Blackpool, the obvious choice, a kind of Lancs Vegas. Only having sampled UK casinos and never having been to Vegas, the gaff was mind-blowing. You can fit England into Oz 60 times, you can fit most English casinos into Burswood Casino, Perth about 600 times. Another lifelong ambition to fulfil, was to sit around a proper poker table, not playing the dealer, but playing against other people.

And so it came to pass. By some fluke and by being extremely lucky, I managed to win a tidy sum. This completely vexed the Aussies in attendance, who all knew the game inside out, and were flummoxed by my tactics. The secret was to not have any and not really have a clue what you were doing. Worked for me.

You got to know when to hold 'em and know when to fold 'em.

The next instalment is to see England fold for the last time tomorrow.

17 December – Day 4 Perth Test
Australia 244 & 527-5 declared
England 219 & 265-5

Only fold they didn't. In fact, for most of the day it looked like a surprise could really be on the cards.

It was quite a bit cooler at the WACA today, for the anticipated death knell of England's Ashes tour. To expect anything less than a convincing Australian win at the start seemed to defy logic. In 1,700 or so Test matches over the years, no team has scored more than 418 to win in the fourth innings. Even at a steady scoring rate England would have the game won if they could last out the two remaining days. A draw seemed the least likely outcome and if England batted the time, they'd probably win the match. For that to occur, something absolutely mental had to happen and against an attack of Warne and McGrath, one of the best spinners ever and one of the best seamers ever (albeit past his best), it seemed as likely as Duncan Fletcher doing slapstick comedy in the Lucky Shag later.

Early on, the more typical English conditions seemed to suit our batsmen, and it was nice to see two of our younger guns doing the business. Cook and Bell were two of those who could be accused of being a timid imitation of the big hitters from when we last won the Ashes. OK, Bell was there, but his contribution pretty negligible.

When they got through to lunch unscathed it was a great achievement. The 'thoroughly professional' Australians were appealing for everything, which you couldn't really blame them for as it had worked on the umpires in the previous Tests. Warne especially was begging, imploring the umpires to give all sorts of wacky decisions. He does seem to push it big time, but it would be a brave match referee who sent him into international retirement with a ban for excessive appealing. All the Englishmen in the ground, Barmy or not, were shouting a mocking 'Howzat' as the histrionics continued.

The Aussies also shout 'catch' when the ball is rolling along the ground or passing through harmlessly to the keeper. I am reliably informed that it is Gilchrist doing the shouting and not Warne. This is disappointing as the theory I was developing was that it was in fact the clicking of Adam Gilchrist's freaky jaw that was posing the problem, thereby giving a noise akin to an edge.

Despite all this we got through to lunch and to be honest nobody knew what to think. After Adelaide the fear of the jinx stalks us all. Everybody there must have said at some stage that at least we wouldn't lose the game, so here most were keeping schtum.

Then came the afternoon session and things were largely the same. In fact as we got to drinks the two players looked increasingly comfortable. The crowd were enthralled for different reasons. The England fans were, especially as most had no doubt already made plans for Day Five. The Aussies, whilst grudgingly admiring the plucky resistance, seemed stunned that the inevitable victory failed to materialise.

Then came the breakthrough. Warne (who else?) snapped up Bell and then a really slow passage of play ensued before Collingwood went as well. Colly didn't have the look of a man who scored a double century in his last Test, it took him 45 balls for his five runs here, and the Adelaide second innings lives on for him it seems.

With half an hour to go England were still only three wickets down, then Glenn McGrath (who else?) decided to go and ruin it by dismissing Cook and night watchman Hoggard in the same over. Cook, without ever looking fluent, played a great innings of pure steadfast determination. This was against the buoyant Aussies on their own patch. Innings like these suggest he's made of the right stuff.

I'd gone over to join the Barmies for the last hour and there was jubilation amongst the home supporters, probably as much to do with relief as anything. I was suddenly 'befriended' by two locals who were desperately trying to string some abuse together but were struggling to form a cogent argument and sentence.

Mindful of the heavy-handed policing, I invited them to come and sit down. Eventually I understood the premise of their sledge. They'd pretty much beaten a world XI. The problem was they had assumed that Panesar and Mahmood weren't English. I asked them where Symonds was from and they thought he was an Aussie. The conversation broke down when I informed them that he's a Brummie, presumably because they thought I was referring to the ACT Brumbies. Hard work.

Australia had probably done enough in the last hour to be able to wrap the game up in the morning. But there were a couple of positives for England.

The number of wickets lost has indeed gradually fallen each day, starting at 12 on Day One, culminating in just four today. If there could be less than five tomorrow, we're in business.

And there is another reason. It may be harsh to say that the Aussies are turning into Yanks, but there are some signs. The whooping and a hollering, the stunningly biased TV coverage and the massive casinos are examples, but today I encountered another one, the lone nut conspiracy theorist. It was all to do with Packer or Murdoch. There was some cynicism in Brisbane about Ricky's failure to enforce the follow on, and it was mooted that TV money was the issue and a three-day game just wouldn't suit the networks. This seemed preposterous and far-fetched in the extreme. What we had now was a new theory. I was stood in a shop queue trying to fight off the imaginative 3-0 angle from yet another gloating Aussie. This quickly passed and then another local, who had witnessed this conversation, decided it was time to offer me some solace. He told me England would definitely draw tomorrow and the Ashes will go to the Final Test in Sydney. James Packer (I think he said) wouldn't allow anything else apparently. Stupidly difficult to believe, but compared with the horror of contemplating the loss of the Ashes, pretty sound really.

A couple of beers in Chris' hotel bar and we bumped into some old guys from up country. They'd travelled around 800 miles for one day's cricket, pretty impressive. 800 miles one way. They were proper old school Aussies, like the ones you might see on

Skippy or something. When I say on *Skippy*, I mean the TV show, not actually trying to ride a kangaroo, that'd be stupid.

It was funny to relate that they saw Perth as a bit of a metropolis, centre of the universe, and just couldn't understand all the funny looking people they saw from different races. One old timer summed it up perfectly, whilst possibly using the most telegraphed punch line of all time. 'I was going to go to China, Japan, Malaysia, Indonesia, you know just to see what the people are like, and then I thought, "aw jeez nah, I'll just go to Perth"'.

Later the plan was to head to the Lucky Shag and watch the Everton and Chelsea game. It was at this stage that I realised why Perth had been so rubbish when I first arrived. Everywhere shuts at 10pm on a Sunday night. So basically, there was only one place to go to watch the footy. Back to Burswood.

The cab drivers in Perth, as with most places in the world, tend to be non-nationals and the guy who took us to the casino was of a similar ilk. He was from Somalia and had been in Perth for 15 years. Having established we were there for the cricket, he started to tell us about his love for his adopted country. 'I love the country,' he said 'Love Australia, support every Australian team in The World Cup, Swimming, Olympics, everything. Except one thing. I hate the cricket team. Cocky arrogant motherfuckers.' No arguments from us on that one.

Having mentioned that there were loads of Everton fans in Oz, this was most prominent in the casino, it was like an Evertonian enclave. When we went 1-0 up the place went nuts. As it turned out it was a thrilling but ultimately heartbreaking game as Frank Lampard and Drogba scored stunning goals to win 3-2. Sport's crap, hate it. Happy to have missed that one. It looked a bit chilly at Goodison.

As is the karmic way of the world, I consoled myself by giving back some, not all, of my poker winnings from the previous night.

Chris and the other lads had watched West Ham beat Man United. So the Everton game and the poker had gone as expected, tomorrow England needed a gravity defying victory like West Ham.

There was a note of caution to sound at this point, 2mm of rain was forecast for tomorrow, so maybe just like Old Trafford last year, a deluge could bail the Aussies out again.

18 December – Day 5 Perth Test
Australia 244 & 527-5 declared
England 219 & 350
Australia won by 206 runs

So what could this day hold? There were only three real possibilities, but the most likely one being a resounding Aussie win. It was a funny feeling walking to the ground, a certain eeriness. I suppose for the burghers of Perth, it was back to work Monday morning, back to reality after the big weekend of the year. For the England fans, it was the fifteenth and maybe last day of clutching at the straws that said we might hold on to the Ashes.

Inside the ground the crowd was pretty disappointing. No doubt the confident Australian public expected things to be wrapped up nicely. At ten quid a pop, it didn't seem a lot to pay to see the almost inevitable regaining of the Ashes. The match situation still suggested that to back England to avoid defeat would be illogical. To have a chance it seemed likely that Flintoff and Pietersen would have to bat amazingly well. When that happens they don't just block it, the ball goes for miles. So they would score at a decent rate. That means that if those two batted for a significant part of the day, and England lasted all day, they would get to the target. So England would score over one hundred runs more than any other team in the history of Test cricket has ever done ever. An England team two down against probably one of the best sides ever. Not going to happen really.

Chris and I took our place right next to the Barmy Army and the gallows humour was being played out. Glenn McGrath joined in by fanning his cricket pants as if to dry them when he was serenaded, to the tune of *She'll Be Coming Round The Mountain When She Comes*; there's a funny smell of piss over there.

The first hour was fun. The weather was once again kind to the visitors so it was pleasant without being too hot or too sunny. Welcome relief. Then Flintoff and Pietersen looked pretty comfortable, with Flintoff especially playing without inhibition, and clocking up a few runs.

Then his wicket was lost and quickly the Aussies rattled through the tail, leaving them tantalisingly on nine wickets as lunch was taken. It was a bit like standing around waiting for a funeral to start, but something else had been on my mind in the morning session. I thought I recognised the bloke in front of me. I was sure it was the third most famous (but easily the most likeable) Alan Smith in football, the former Crystal Palace manager. It was hard to know how to confirm this suspicion. My mate also thought it was him, but I didn't know how to tackle this. It wouldn't have made much sense to say "Are you you? You are aren't you?"

So I went for "'Scuse me mate, you are either Alan Smith or you sound and look a hell of a lot like him." He enigmatically replied 'I used to be him' and we started having a chat. It sounds a bit twee now to say that all celebs were pleasant on the trip. Actually they were all civil, but Alan was genuinely nice. What a great fella. He happily swapped stories about previous England tours he'd been on but we wanted some football dirt from him. He had Blackpool stories for Chris and some classic Howard Kendall anecdotes for me. He gave us an insight into working for some colourful chairmen at Palace, one of them is actually orange (my words not his) and his account of Alex Ferguson's reaction to the Cantona incident (Alan was the Palace manager at the time) was hilarious. He also talked openly about that 4-3 semi-final win against Liverpool and the Cup Final against United in 1990.

What was unusual about him was that he really listened, and seemed far too genial to be a football manager. You could imagine him being a brilliant assistant, showing genuine empathy. In fact, genuine is the word.

An honour and a privilege to meet him.

Back on the pitch, and the moment happened pretty quickly. It seemed somehow fitting that Shane Warne should get the wicket and Monty should be his victim. One man who had probably the most significant impact on the series, and one man who didn't get chance to do just that until it was too late.

The scenes at the end were understandably joyous, with the Aussie players getting together in a big huddle of celebration. England players Pietersen and Monty waited patiently, as if outside the headmaster's office, not really wanting to knock on the door and disturb. Again it was Warne who showed his class, being the first one over to shake hands with the England pair.

The England supporters magnanimously stood to acclaim the Aussies, and this was taken in the spirit it was intended. The Australian players respectfully applauded back. Matthew Hayden took the time to shake hands with all the Australian 'Fanatics', just a shame there were only about ten of them.

Then Adam Gilchrist came running over. He decided it would be a good time to goad the England fans, cupping his (no-one actually believes they are his) ears to us and giving it the big one. This was pretty unseemly and out of keeping with the general good nature of the occasion. It seems odd that Gilchrist of all the Aussie players chose to do this, McGrath, Warne and Lee, for example, would have loads more reason to do so but just displayed more dignity.

It may have been that he was saying 'just look at the state of these ears'. It's possible. I remember watching the news ages ago where a human ear was being grown on the back of a mouse. Even that looked less out of place than those things Gilchrist had unceremoniously placed on the side of his head. Maybe people who've travelled several thousand miles deserve better, maybe not. But it was noticeable that he was the only one who saw fit to act like this, thus placing himself on the top of everybody's 'Wanker list'.

Well done Adam.

As it turned out, he wasn't the only one who embarrassed himself today.

Afterwards it was that sinking feeling and the realisation that we'd blown it, nothing left to play for. We'd lost 3&2, and there was nothing we could do.

For the third consecutive Test Match Day Five, it was time to go to the pub. I'm a bit discomfited to say that I was spoiling for an argument with an Aussie, and to be honest you really don't have to wait too long for a suitable opportunity. There were about four of our group in the pub having a few drinks and Chris found a stray mobile phone. As it was ringing, he thought it would be a good idea to answer it, thereby providing a clue as to the owner.

What he got was a load of abuse, accusing him of stealing the phone and threatening all sorts of retribution if he didn't give it back. The problem was that the other person on this call was only about ten yards away, so it was a case of wandering over. He thought it'd be good to change the conversation to cricket not really a favourite subject at that moment.

I somewhat spitefully shook his hand and said 'Well done on winning the Ashes mate, you deserved it. I'm especially pleased that you won it here in Perth, coz fuck all else ever happens here'. He struggled with this for a bit and then objected. It was a rubbish argument as we were both drunk but when he cited the Boat Race

136

(I think he meant the America's Cup) I reminded him that we held that in the UK and that the same two teams always get to the final.

This lame argument continued for seemingly ages, with us spending a bit of time just staring at each other. There was a moment when I thought he might throw a punch and he probably felt that same way. Thank God that didn't happen.

I was reliably informed later in the evening that I had said 'What's the music scene like round here?' to him over and over again. The shame.

There can't be many worse places to be on the losing side than in Australia.

19 December

"I wanted to send you a message thanking you for your support over the past couple of weeks. (This) was a very daunting and excit-ing task all at once, very bittersweet indeed. Through all the nerves, your words of support……..have been really overwhelming and encouraging."

This was a pretty moving speech made during the Third Test.

Anyway, enough about the new Yellow Wiggle, it's time to reflect on the loss of The Ashes.

Brisbane was an ambush. England were under-prepared, under-cooked and Down Under, a Test match defeat waiting to happen. The Second Test was the turning point; it was heartbreaking to watch a team that held the ascendancy for four days, completely blow it on Day Five. They could have come to Perth with some serious confidence even if they'd only snatched a draw, but alas no.

England had major chances in Adelaide and Perth but just couldn't press home the advantage. Annoying as it was to admit, Australia had better bowlers, better batsmen and better fielders.

England had made three decent totals and three sub-standard ones. Even if they'd put two of these together in the same Test, they'd probably only be looking at 2-0 now and the series would be just alive.

There are really only two things for England to play for. Somehow salvage my bet and stop Warne getting his 700th on his home ground, Perth set things up perfectly with him tantalisingly placed on 699. The other thing they must do is avoid a 5-0 drubbing. It seems a pity that this is a possibility as so many inferior England sides have toured Australia and been spared that indignity. It's going to take some doing.

It's off to Melbourne tomorrow and despite my bravado about how the Australians would react to being 3-0 down I can't pretend that I'm really looking forward to it. It's a strange feeling being away from home for ages and the two remaining cities and cricket grounds are ones I've visited before. The wide-eyed fascination has gone.

Without craving bad news, if somebody called and said you've got to go home, I'd be willing to do it. Nothing else to say. That's it for today.

Victoria:
The Garden State,
The Place To Be,
On The Move

"If you think you can win, you can win. Faith is necessary to victory."

WILLIAM HAZLITT
(ENGLISH ESSAYIST)

20 December - Arrive Melbourne

Alas it was goodbye to Perth, a lovely place. You could easily see why so many people who leave the UK choose that part of the world. Sadly, once again I had managed to visit a place without seeing anything outside the city.

Having said that, it's hard to compete with the Aussies who really don't think that much of travelling long distances for relatively short stays. Several Western Australians mentioned that I had to visit the Margaret River. Travel time? Five hours. Not really day-trip material.

Notably loads of Australia supporters at the cricket at all three Tests had travelled hundreds of miles to be there. I remember once getting a train from Leeds to watch cricket at Egbaston and couldn't believe how long it took. I immediately swore (and quickly broke) an oath to never travel that far again for a cricket match.

So it was time for yet another internal flight and I must admit to having a moment of guilt in terms of my part in adding to the big hole in the ozone layer above Australia. That was the bad news. So what's the good news I hear you cry? Well, my copious purchasing of Factor 30 plus had actually qualified me for a Nivea Beach Ball. Nice that.

Back to the environment and an expert has recently predicted that Australia needs to cut internal flights by 96% to prevent further damage to the environment. Back home, the legendary (but slightly morose) Thom Yorke of Radiohead has suggested that the concept of a world tour may cease because of the carbon emissions from flying. Planting Fake Plastic Trees won't make any difference to that.

As I approached Victoria's state capital I reflected that the cities I have visited so far have all been pretty sedate and had a laid back vibe, more so than any English city you could name. In fact, they really had the feel of large towns rather than bustling municipalities. Melbourne is totally different to this.

This place was totally buzzing and as I was located right in the centre, the pace was relentless. Melbourne feels like a world city and apart from the rapidity of life, the cosmopolitan nature is totally out of keeping with my earlier sleepier bases. It also feels more like a place where you have to keep your wits about you; such is the sheer volume of people out and about.

Crossing the road is pretty hazardous too. As well as the bustling streets of cars, buses, lorries and bikes, there is the added complication of trams to look out for too. I had a near-miss within hours of arriving. Being mowed down by a tram in an Alan Bradley stylee would be the ultimate indignity for someone from

Blackpool. It's like trying to negotiate getting over the road in Amsterdam, with one notable difference.

Speaking of drugs, there is a massive breaking news story today and it refers to one of the most famous Victorians around. It has been announced that one Shane Keith Warne will quit playing for Australia after the Sydney Test. It seems as though the rest of the tour will revolve around the man they call 'The Chic of Tweak' and 'The Earl of Twirl'.

Fittingly he will play his penultimate Test at his home ground, the immense MCG and this will almost certainly see him become the first cricketer ever to take 700 Test wickets (and finally put my stupidly optimistic bet to bed). It may again be one of those painful moments where part of you thinks that it really is great to be there to witness history; the other half of you would prefer it not to be happening at all.

His final Test will take place in Sydney at the SCG, where he began his Test career in January 1992, starting with the unspectacular bowling figures of 1-150. According to the TV news, it appears extremely likely that a similar announcement from fellow England destroyer Glenn McGrath will follow shortly.

It seems really odd that the next time England face Australia in the Ashes in 2009, neither of these players will be taking part. Many will find this sad news, personally I can't wait.

In an attempt to get myself fired up for the rest of the trip, I had a read of the Aussie Fanatics songbook, Six, Jugs and Rock n Roll. Now it would be easy to dismiss the Fanatics as a pallid imitation of the Barmy Army and to reject their attempts at writing songs as puerile and pathetic. Easy and totally valid. In fairness, some of the Barmy stuff isn't exactly grown up but compared to this crap it's Stephen Hawking-like in its intellectual insight. Thinking about it, Professor Hawking would add a certain tunefulness to the Aussie singing.

The best (or rather worst) example is a song called 'Are you ever gonna wash, pommie.' This is supposedly sung to the tune of *Rock DJ* by Robbie Williams and here's a snippet

Wash your hands when you've been to the can
Should you wash it?
(yes you can)
We smell
(skunk)
You smell
(skunk)
You've got body odour
I've got the soap
Gonna rub it on your back
It's time to wash your body

Yeah right.
A few thoughts

1. The notion that English people don't wash from a country with a drought issue is interesting
2. Using a Robbie Williams song (and an especially lame one even by the Potteries crooner's own low standards) for a chant is just plain wrong
3. Er, this seems a trifle elaborate lyrically for a group of fans who struggle with the complex words to 'Aussie Aussie Aussie, Oi Oi Oi'
4. 'Gonna rub it on your back,' extremely liberal for your average homophobic Aussie cricket fan.

Other than that, the rest of it is utter garbage. I may be wrong but the whole Fanatics thing seems a choreographed and contrived attempt to match the Barmy Army. The difference appears to be that the Army is a spontaneous celebration of watching sport. I know they are not everyone's cup of tea but at least it's a bit of a laugh and win, lose or draw, the team appreciate the support. Some of the patter is genuinely funny, and you hear authentic laughter from the English and Aussies in the ground when the Barmies are in full flight.

The Fanatics 'phenomenon' seems more like what happened in Australia when the British Lions toured and many of the visitors wore the red Lions shirt, making it look pretty distinctive and illustrating just what a high proportion of the crowd were British. The Australian solution? Issue garish canary yellow T-shirts to the home fans. Tres imaginative.

Anyway after getting slightly irritated by all this I decided that I'm going to enjoy Melbourne and Sydney and soak up the rest of the tour. Seven weeks is quite a long time to be away from home but I realised that making a trip like this is really a 'once in a lifetime' opportunity so it would be absurd to sulk about the cricket. Every Test match is a huge occasion in Oz and the Boxing Day Test is one of THE sporting traditions in Australia and it's only a few days away.

So tomorrow it's up and at 'em.

21 December

Out and about in Melbourne and the throbbing metropolis seemed to go about its business in the normal manner. But today was a very different day for one main reason; over at the MCG Shane Warne finally confirmed that he was retiring from Test cricket.

There is no denying that he has been the biggest character in cricket during my lifetime, and despite all the controversy in his private life, he comes over as being quite an OK geezer really. You've got to say his career has been spectacular, and the TV here keep showing probably the most extravagant moment, when he bowled Mike Gatting with what was dubbed 'the Ball of the Century.' It was amazing, the ball turning at such an acute angle that it should have probably indicated before it turned left. Gatt's reaction was dignified and understated, the resigned look of a man who'd just been told he had to pay a 20p fine because his library book was late.

Perhaps somewhat predictably Graham Gooch was quoted as saying "if it had been a cheese roll, it would never have got passed him." Quite.

The Australian media are rightly celebrating a glittering career; my own personal memory of Warne is a slightly quirky one but maybe illustrates the fact that he is a winner. He was playing in a one-dayer at Old Trafford and England had bowled Australia out for pretty low total, and it looked as though we were odds on to win the game. An hour or so later, usual service was resumed and havoc had typically been reeked; England were five wickets down with only 40-odd runs on the board.

You may not believe this but there was rain in the air that day in Manchester, and the Aussies were full of it in the field, running around trying to get the minimum number of overs in for a valid match to take place. This involved the usually leisurely Warne jogging back to his mark, and England's Paul Collingwood trying to take as much time as possible between deliveries.

Warne glowered at Colly and said "Are you ready?" and managed to look and sound sarcastic, patronising, belittling, angry, and pitying at the same time. Basically he was using his 'legend' status to undermine a young man making his way in the dog-eat-dog world of international cricket. Warne seemed indestructible, imperious and ruthlessly professional in a situation like this. He was totally determined to win, and if this meant undermining an opponent, no blahddy warries mate.

What is interesting is that even in his home state of Victoria Warne is not universally loved by any means. In conversation with the locals, you don't have to wait long for someone to call him a 'sleazebag' or words to that effect, again comment on his private life rather than his cricket. Maybe this is the Aussie version of 'tall poppy syndrome', or in this case 'slightly podgy poppy with blond highlights syndrome.'

From a personal point of view this bloke seems determined to ruin my cricketing life. Here are just a few of his atrocities so far, he has...

1) Ensured that Australia have dominated cricket and more especially England for about 15 years.

2) Helped Australia to win World Cups from seemingly impossible situations.

3) Butchered my last trip to Oz by making his comeback in the final Test and helping Australia to a series victory.

4) Presided over the 'Disaster of Adelaide'.

5) Almost certainly ruined my bet

And many, many more. Now he's going to jack in playing for the Aussies, for Victoria and even for his club side St. Kilda. So of course that means he won't be playing for Hampshire, right? Not a bit of it. He has decided to spend two more years in county cricket, captaining Hants. I'm no Nostradamus, but I can see a scenario in which my beloved Lancashire are on the brink of winning their first County Championship for 80-odd years and then he comes along and scuppers it. Nothing more certain. Basically, if playing your home games in Manchester's gloomy microclimate doesn't get you, Warnie will.

Speaking of domestic cricket, it's totally bizarre to watch the slightly unedifying spectacle of Australian state cricket on the TV. It's a well known fact that one man and his dog watch county cricket in England, but to play a domestic game at the MCG which holds around 100,000 just looks weird. You would have thought that the games would be taken around the states but apparently not. Anyway, there is a bit of controversy around the MCG right now.

Yesterday's game between bitter rivals Victoria and New South Wales was a low scoring affair. The problem according to the players was the pitch, and the 'G' as it's known round here, is one of the venues which uses a drop-in pitch, presumably to allow all the other sport to go on without ruining the playing surface. This is a big deal over here, especially with the Boxing Day Test attracting such massive crowds. The curator (groundsman to you and me) is getting hassle from all angles, but is currently unavailable for comment. One of the players from yesterday's game was quoted as saying it's the worst MCG pitch he has ever seen.

So it looks like England to win in two days at the moment then.

22 December

Australian Test retirees are like buses at the moment. They are smelly, unhygienic and driven by idiots. Sorry, scratch that. You wait absolutely ages for one and then two come along at once. The inevitable announcement of Glenn McGrath's retirement has followed in a low-key (compared to Warnie) manner today.

The difference is that McGrath will take part in the World Cup, no doubt leading Australia to a spectacular victory, thereby rounding off his career in a picture book way.

On a one-day theme, England's squad for the Tri-Nations series poses a serious number of questions and leaves you with one single impression, they've completely lost it. First the unavoidable, Steve Harmison has announced his retirement from one day cricket. Maybe those 14-ball overs have taken their toll (sorry) and just maybe he wasn't going to be selected anyway, who knows?

The wicket-keeping situation appears even more confusing, with Geraint Jones finally completing the painful journey from hero to zero, and not even figuring in the squad. Presumably this means that Chris Read will play in the Boxing Day Test, but that's pure speculation. Probably depends whether we use Guinevere and set of balls number six to select our team.

Mike Yardy, he of the comedic batting stance, who played all through the recent ICC Trophy, doesn't get a look in which makes sense to me but makes you wonder why he's been persevered with in the past. Also, the man who supposedly couldn't bat or field at the start of the series, one Mudhudsen Singh Panesar, makes the cut. Oh yeah, and there's no captain. Michael Vaughan is in the squad, but as chairman of selectors David Graveney cryptically stated 'it would not be appropriate to announce the captaincy of the one-day side at this stage.' What even when you've named the squad Dave?

My hunch is that if Vaughan is fit Freddie will be on the first plane home and get his injury sorted out.

Speaking of injury, it looks as though I had added it to insult for my Aussie blog readers. All I did was examine the relative records of Warne and Muralitharan.

It is widely accepted that Warne is one of the best cricketers of all time, indeed he was named as one of Wisden's 'Five cricketers of the 20th century,' powerful stuff. His appearance, lifestyle and general exuberance make him a journalist's dream. English spectators have seen him in his pomp and he is also, probably quite rightly, credited with bringing spin-bowling, most especially leg-spin, out of the doldrums. He is stereotypically Australian in so many ways, and that's an insult and a compliment at the same time.

Murali isn't famed for tabloid headlines, and there has been loads of controversy about his action, which has once again been cleared. It is fair to say that some of the evidence points to the Sri Lankan being a better bowler, such as:

Better average
Better strike rate
More five wicket hauls despite having played less Tests

There is of course an argument to say Murali has played against weaker opposition. And a counter-argument to say that Warne never had to play against the best team in the world, name-ly Australia. Warnie's never been called for chucking as far as I know, and I'm pretty sure that Muttiah has never been banned for taking drugs, or accused of taking cash from Indian bookies.

Anyway, the Australians seem completely indignant at the suggestion that anyone could live up to their Shane. I think this argument needs further discussion when I get to the 'G' on Boxing Day. Let's see if I can elicit a reaction.

Back to Warnie, it was interesting to note that Ian Chappell helped counsel him in terms of timing his departure correctly. You'd have to say it was impeccable in terms of going out at the top, just after avenging a surprise defeat to your greatest rivals. Chappell seems to have a bit of a tough guy reputation out here, and it was revealing to read some quotes from the Lillee/Thomson era, when his team talks appear to have been "Boycott? Bounce the c**t, Edrich? Bounce the c**t," when preparing his quick bowlers to face England's batsmen.

The incongruence here is that for someone my age the Chappell name only conjures up one real memory, the decision by Trevor Chappell, encouraged by brother and captain Greg, to bowl the last ball of a one-dayer at the MCG underarm so the New

Zealanders couldn't hit the ball for six. I'm sure this was deemed to be especially un-Australian and seems like the antithesis to the Aussie edict of 'backing yourself'. Ian remains the archetypal tough guy, and just loved a beer apparently. I think he's the one who said something along the lines of if you only managed 48 beers in the Australia to England flight you'd be virtually classed as a teetotaller in his day. Hope you had your flight socks on Ian?

Having spent a bit of time off the ale, I decide it's time to get back in the saddle and head down to PJ O'Briens, the Barmy pub for Melbourne, and have a few drinks, it is Friday night after all. I spot another Evertonian I know, a lad who sits about four seats from me at Goodison, and see a few familiar faces from the other Tests. There are thousands more England fans expected for the attractive Christmas/New Year Melbourne/Sydney combo, it must be devastating to come out with the Ashes over already. That said, PJ's is buzzing and along with Chris I get a few down me then head for the Crown Casino.

This makes Perth's Super Casino look small really and reminds me of a conversation I had in the crowd at the Third Test. I was boring someone shitless about the sheer magnitude of the Burswood Casino when a complete stranger turned round and said, 'it's tiny.' I thought they were joking and they left me with the barbed comment 'wait till you get to Melbourne.' Well now I had and I could see exactly what they meant. This place was obscene.

It was back to the poker table for me and an average night on the green baize. My main sport was chatting to the locals about cricket and then state just how much I was "looking forward to seeing the last goodbye to the second best spin bowler in the world," and seeing how many milliseconds it took the Aussies to bite. I tried to suffix the word 'statistically' to my statement, but didn't even get to the end of the sssss sound at the start.

They are really just sssssoooo ssssensitive round here.

23 December

It's Christmas time, there's no need to be afraid. At least it felt a bit more like Christmas today; it pissed it down.

On the subject of piss, the man seemingly afraid today was Glenn McGrath. Looking very nervous in his press conference, it seems odd that this slightly shy, uneasy figure is the one who dishes out the verbals on the cricket pitch. What also seems totally mad is that the Aussies don't have a Test Match for eleven months. Can anyone remember England ever going that long without a Test? It seems to be making it a really easy decision for the older players to turn it in. Well that and giving England a proper shoe-ing anyway.

From a purely English point of view it'd be good to see them all knock it on the head just to give us half a chance right now.

A pet phrase in Australia is to refer to 'whingeing poms.' They just love saying that. They may have a point, but we would struggle to compete with the amount of bleating they have done about getting knocked out of the 2006 World Cup by Italy. Watching a TV interview it was curious to hear the penalty offender, Blackburn defender Lucas Neill, managing to keep a straight face when he said the Australians were "a little bit too honest and were brought up to play by the rules." Who said the Aussies can't do comedy? Maybe it was me.

Not sure Lucas is viewed as a bastion of fair play amongst his fellow professionals in England. Whether it was a penalty or not is debatable, but he must know that being a centre-half is much the same as being in the mosh pit, you don't go to ground unless it is absolutely necessary. And then you take someone with you if possible.

The TV show then went on to make the typically one-eyed point that had Australia won that game, they would have made their way seamlessly to the semis as they would have only played Ukraine in the Quarters. Maybe, maybe not.

Because I was missing out on my staple diet of two games of five-a-side football per week, it was time to get some exercise. This came in the shape of another bike ride, this time down by the Yarra River, and it's a pretty picturesque route. My mate at the hire shop, who incidentally hated Shane Warne and thought he was a proper scumbag, had recommended a 10 miles or so trip to a waterfall. After a few miles, you are right out in the sticks and I was having a pleasant time, indulging myself in a little ipod inspired sing-song, when I saw a sign urging caution as there may be snakes around. I was only about two miles from my ultimate destination so there really seemed only one noble thing to do.

So I did the opposite and turned back. When I was at Australia Zoo I had a bash at holding a snake and had come to the following conclusions; they were heavier than I thought, smoother than I thought and they still scared the life out of me. Whingeing Pom indeed.

It was back to PJ's again tonight and the place was buzzing with visitors and Aussies alike. The Barmy Army were the big story in town and all sorts of people wanted to get involved. Nice that.

As I meandered my way home, news came through that Everton had pulled off an unlikely win at Reading.

The world's a happy place once again.

24 December

Andrew Flintoff has come out publicly today to stress the importance of putting on a good show for the England fans who have made the trip. "They have supported us over the last three games, it would be nice to give them something back." A few grand would be nice Freddie, but even a draw in either of the last two Tests would be bearable.

On the Australian side Shane Warne has continued to display great decorum and dignity by going on about 'having the wood' over Ian Bell, and referring to him as the Shermanator, apparently a character from the movie American Pie. Great areas Shane, professional to the end, if a tad puerile.

I decide to get on my bike and this time head down to St Kilda, the very area where it all began for Shane Warne. The place seemed pretty quiet, not a big shock on Christmas Eve, but seemed like a classic seaside town/suburb really. Pretty similar to Blackpool, a few less rides at the Amusement Park, maybe one or two more palm trees. This reminded me of St Helens and Great Britain's Rugby League player Leon Pryce, who caused a bit of a stir recently with his quote about Australia: "It's not all it's made out to be (in Bondi). All the Aussies come over and say how good it is, but I'd much rather be back in Bradford. I'd rather be on Blackpool beach than Bondi Beach. They can keep the country to themselves."

Nice one Leon, Bondi and Blackpool beach are most definitely different.

After cycling around for a bit I happened upon a pub with the cockneyest name ever, Elephant and Wheelbarrow, and decide to slide in there for a bit of refreshment. As I had a footy shirt on, I was accosted by a Bolton lad who I got chatting to about football, cricket and all things Australian. It is probably part of the Peter Kay/Dave Spikey phenomenon, but I now sincerely believe that everyone from Bolton sounds funny, even when they are not trying to be.

This was reinforced by a taxi ride I once took to the Reebok Stadium, where the driver was telling me about his son working as a policeman in Burnley, which he described as "Just like Bay Root." Anyway, it turned out these lads were pretty funny, although they seemed to have a stock phrase "it's all about the bushy gash," which is a bit of a new one on me. They were off to the Barmy Army

Christmas party tomorrow, so I arranged to meet up with them again there.

I'd probably had more Stella than a cyclist really should have, but managed to make my way back into the city unscathed, having worked off a decent thirst.

It still feels odd being away from home at Christmas. I can definitely see the appeal for people who decide to go abroad at this time of year to get away from the weather, the drudgery or maybe just the whole routine and rigmarole, but I figure I should definitely be at home really. It makes me feel a little insignificant in a massive city where I hardly know anyone, and in a sense I'll be glad when tomorrow is out of the way and it's back to the cricket.

At least tomorrow sees the day when I finally get to open the Christmas present from my parents that I've been lugging around since I left Manchester over a month ago. I asserted that I would wait until Christmas Day to open it, even though I was given the pretty non-cryptic clue that it was 'something you will be able to use while you are over there'. As I am a recent convert to the 'number one all over' look, it was blindingly obvious they'd got me some hair clippers, but I didn't really have the heart to break that news to them. I didn't want to ruin the 'surprise.'

The eeriness of Xmas continued for me as I made my way out for a few more bevvies tonight. I wasn't really in the mood as everyone else seemed jubilant. Then they played that tune, you know the *Fairytale of New York*, a classic number and probably the one bittersweet song that characterises Christmas. Maybe this is a time of year for excessive introspection, or maybe that's just me, but this song just makes me think about the world and the stuff what's in it. Or, more correctly, my world and the stuff in that.

So I decided that really I'm just forcing it, and chose to head back to the hotel, in a slightly maudlin and melancholic state, and rest up ready for the big party tomorrow.

25 December

So this is Christmas, and what have you done?

Well the first thing is that I've been unwittingly duped by my parents. Having put off my weekly haircut, safe in the knowledge that I'd be doing my own for the first time, the 'mystery' gift indeed proved to be mysterious. Some binoculars no less. Ideal for use at the cricket but not specifically designed for self-use with a patented 180 degree rotating head as I was expecting. Never mind, I'm not exactly a hippie anyway, those days are gone my friend.

A quick bike ride to blow the cobwebs away, and I was caught in a deluge by Melbourne's famous weather. Seriously, when it rains here, it really goes for it. My last Melbourne trip was blighted by rain, with the entire Boxing Day's play being lost. This resulted in 70,000 people turning up to watch non-stop precipitation.

Anyway, the flip side of Melbourne is that the weather can soon take a turn for the better too and within minutes bright sunshine was the prevalent climate. It just felt even weirder as I mooched down to a Christmas party in my shorts and in the sunshine. Even odder is that I was on my own. Chris had headed up to see his mate somewhere a few miles from Melbourne so it's just little (but steadily getting bigger) old me.

The location of Birrarung Marr, just off Federation Square in the City Centre and beside the Yarra River, was an ideal venue. A vast open space on a dusty, grassless surface seemed perfect and the vibe upon arrival was like walking into a music festival. There could only really be one thing to scupper it, bucketfuls of rain.

The party set up was a bit odd where you had to buy drinks tickets from one booth and then hand them over at the bar to get a bevvy. I first witnessed this type of system in Millennium Square Leeds, which has recently opened up to host outdoor gigs. Home favourites The Kaiser Chiefs attracted a massive attendance and the crowd got well out of hand. The beer tent nearly went over and carrying more than three drinks proved to be an *It's a Knockout* style experience. You could almost hear Stuart 'a bit too zany for his own good' Hall in the background shouting, "Just look at the Belgians!"

This time it was a little more civilised, with the bar queues quite limited, for a rather curious reason. Hundreds of people had formed a queue across the middle of the venue and were waiting for what seemed like a tiny kiosk. You could immediately see that whatever they were after, they were going to be waiting for hours, so it must have been seriously worthwhile.

You'll never guess what happened.

It absolutely lashed it down. It was raining dingos and whatever the Aussie feline equivalent is. Luckily for me - and let's face it this hadn't been the most fortunate trip to date - I was in the process of getting a festive glass of red wine and was handily ensconced in a beer tent. Perfect timing. Peering out of my shelter, the rain was so hard that visibility was limited. There's something quite comforting about being in a tent (at least a secure one) when the rain is really pouring. You are kind of safe and living on the edge as well, just a little bit of canvass between you and the elements.

As the rain abated a little, two thoughts immediately occurred. This scene was just like the Glastonbury festival the first time it rained, no-one had really prepared for it, and everyone was dressed wholly inappropriately. The other was to pity the poor folk in that queue. They admirably stood their ground throughout the second biblical onslaught of the tour (Gilchrist's was the first) and just waited. It appears that they were waiting to collect their tickets for the following day. It seemed likely that some of them would only just have arrived in Oz, what a welcome.

It's a funny old place is Melbourne, it can look pristine and magnificent when the sun shines. Conversely, like most places, when it rains it just looks grim.

155

Even by the admission of the Barmies, the food was seriously ropey at the party but that didn't seem to matter as plenty of drinks were downed and typical of the spirit of the England fans, there was a major singsong. There were also thousands of people at the party, thereby emphasising the magnitude of the Barmy Army. There is some serious earning power there, but somehow you get the impression that it's run on a volunteer rather than business footing, and most people do it for the crack not for the cash.

And, of course, as it was a Barmy party there were TV cameras galore, continuing the inquisitive Australian sycophancy towards the Army.

I bumped into the Bolton lads again, you know, the 'bushy gash' boys, and hung around with them. At some stage in the early evening I had a chat with my family back home, it's fair to say that they got even less sense out of me than usual. They are used to me having a bit of a hangover at 8am on Christmas morning, not being completely wasted (I did have 11 hours start on them like).

The night took us back to PJ O'Briens and I converted my post-Test getting hammered habit into a pre-Test habit. The last memory I have of the evening was downing Jaegy-bombs. This horrible concoction is made by dropping a shot of Jaegermeister (ruthlessly efficient German herbal liqueur) into a glass of Red Bull (20 cups of coffee in a can) and the results are memorable. Well, actually not memorable in the slightest.

For the first time on the trip I'd failed to do my blog because I was just far too bevvied.

Merry Christmas everyone.

26 December – Day 1 Melbourne Test
England 159
Australia 48-2

Victoria: The Garden State

The insipid local band Crowded House probably wrote their ingratiating (but sadly catchy) *Four Seasons in One Day* about Melbourne. The weather in this place is as unpredictable as England's inferiority is painfully and eminently predictable.

I awoke with a different type of hangover, the one unique to a night imbibing drinks laced with excessive caffeine. It's a weird, spaced-out feeling, and all in all is not wholly unpleasant. It's probably comparable to that brief euphoric spell you have when you've not slept, just prior to the dramatic slump.

First thing in the morning and it was raining. It really does seem to do that a lot in Melbourne, and as I met up with Chris we decided to go and get some breakfast on the way to the 'G', there was no prospect of play for a bit. Sadly, it was an indictment on how the tour had gone that I felt reasonably happy with the weather. England's only remaining role in the Series was that of party pooper. There were four parties to go to in the next two weeks; Warnie's 700th, Glenn's Leaving Do, Shane's Retirement and The Whitewash. I'd already shelled out a few quid to get my invite to these but didn't really feel in the party mood.

The only team news was the inclusion of wicket–keeper Read ahead of Jones, but this really felt like closing the stable door after the horse had bolted some years previously and then died of old age, and the hinges on the door had rusted over. Suddenly the weather cleared and we were caught high and dry with a full fry-up as play began. We needn't have worried. This was quickly despatched and after a short cab ride we were there. Such was England's batting paralysis, we missed 20 mins of play, which meant we were in the fifth over. The scoring rate exactly mimicked the respective currencies of the two countries;

$2.50 = £1
5 overs = 2 runs.
Dull.

Ashes To Dust

I started to feel more delicate so what I yearned for was a decent seat with a bit of a breather from the Aussie onslaught. Maybe I felt a little bantered out for a little while.

Unfortunately I assumed my preordained position on the front row of the fourth tier at the MCG, a nausea inducing seat if ever I had one, wondering what treats were in store. The 'G' itself was a somewhat disappointing three quarters full, the weather having dampened the spirits really. It had been hoped (and widely speculated) that the record of 90,800 for the West Indies' visit in 1960 would be broken.

Having bemoaned the crowd (and everything else) you have to say that the MCG is magnificent. The biggest cricket ground in England is Lords and holds around 30,000. This would look like a Subbuteo Cricket ground next to the 'G', which as well as holding 100,000 also has a massive playing area, with all run fours a regular occurrence. On my last visit eight years ago, I marvelled at the size of the Great Southern Stand, which is a four-tier structure stretching around the boundary of half of the playing area and holds 48,000. This was my home for today. The other half was a bit of a hotch-potch back then, but the 2006 Commonwealth Games gave the sports mad city of Melbourne a chance to do what they seem to love to do best, build a behemoth for sport. So the Great Southern Stand is now outshone by its opposite number. Despite the new stand being one complete structure, different sections have different names honouring some greats of the past.

I think it was former Aussie fast bowler Geoff Lawson who was speculating that if the Great Southern stand is so called, then the other could be the Flaming Great Northern Stand or even the Blahddy Great Northern Stand. Like it.

So now it's a slightly ill-fitting stadium of two halves (you can see the join), but it's still amazing. T h e re isn't an outpouring of noise in the ground, but a constant hum or buzz. The lay-out means that the sound doesn't really have anywhere to go. Because of the size of the playing surface and the height of the stands, you don't feel as engaged in the action, you are a distant spectator in a sense, so it's not the usual 'oohs' and 'aahs' of a cricket match, it appears somehow more sedate. Maybe it was the stop-start nature of play, we did have two rain breaks in the morning after play had started, or the ubiquitous hangovers, but the atmosphere was a little subdued up to lunch.

Having stated just how unpredictable the weather is in Melbourne, the short-range forecast is easy. A couple of minutes before it rains, a kind of chill pervades the air, the temperature tangibly drops by a few degrees and just after you've had time to mention it to your neighbour, the rain begins. Spooky that, adding to the surreal vibe of the day so far.

My desire for a quiet life was answered by the feeling of cruel fate mocking me as the noise of a relentless and burly Tasmanian rang around my ears. This was to be my next seat neighbour for the day. We were both big lads and not really designed to squeeze into seats this size. That didn't help and his constant chatter accentuated my feeling of dread. He started his assault by asking me if I wished my grandfather had stolen some bread so I'd have been an Aussie and so the onslaught began. This line of questioning continued until he told me about the hundreds of English female back packers he'd shagged and then I had to object.

This bloke wasn't exactly a looker, and had a ginger goatee beard. Now I'm certainly not gingist, I've actually been to Gingistan and the people are lovely, but if you are sporting a ginger goatee, it probably doesn't bode well for what was underneath. "Yeah mate," I spouted, "course you did, and then you woke up."

Unfortunately, I had meant this in a playground 'in your dreams' or maybe 'Growing a (ginger) beard' type way. Sadly he majorly misinterpreted it. He thought it meant I was going to knock him out.

Fighting talk misunderstanding number one. The next one followed quickly when a bloke with teeth like burnt chips gave me a volley of 'Pommie Bastard' based abuse. 'You got any dentists here mate,' I asked. My intention, give it a rest you fluoride free tosser. His interpretation, I wanted to knock his teeth out. I've had better days.

I think that particular 'friend' got booted out later, I wasn't the only target for his ire. Good riddance there but once the confusion was sorted with my Tasmanian Devil, we had a good laugh with him and his mates.

Back to the 'action', England limped along in the morning, reaching 36-1 by lunch, but this was an hors d'oevre really. The main course was Warnie and his quest to get his 700th. The sub-plot of when he would bowl, or rather, the main storyline, was played up nicely by the Aussies, as a couple of false starts took place. One involved the Aussie leg spinner having his cap removed by a team-mate (it was one of the little ones, probably Langer) as if to hand it to the umpire, and then sticking it back on. It was a nice bit of panto really; it is the season after all. Andrew Symonds probably took the pantomime spirit a little too far with his make-up and wig combo though. It was the English-born (did I mention he's English?) all-rounder who briefly took on the role of villain when he was brought onto bowl before the crowd favourite.

And then it was Warnie-time.

The crowd stood to acclaim their hero, the police and stewards made a ring between the boundary rope and the fans to prevent any over-enthusiastic sorts running on. The sense of anticipation was palpable, and the problem for the England fans in the ground was that this was like death and taxes, an absolute stone-cold certainty, clearly a matter of 'when' not 'if.' Even if Warnie had got a serious injury out there, as long as he still had one leg to stand on you know he would have been out there until the 700th was in the bag.

Victoria: The Garden State

The noise levels lifted dramatically when Shane made his way to his mark. The opening day of the Boxing Day Test is THE big day on the Aussie cricket calendar. The locals understandably wanted to say 'I was there' and were impatient for Warnie to reach this milestone. His early overs were full of the usual 'catch-its', but the breakthrough wasn't coming easily.

The next milestone was actually Andrew Strauss' first half-century of the series. As he was quite possibly the unluckiest man in Australia this tour, it was nice to see. Next, Brett Lee got in on the act by getting Collingwood out.

It wouldn't be long now. Earlier, and this may have been wishful thinking on my part, I'm sure Adam Gilchrist missed a couple of opportunities to play a part in the 700th. I'm sure it happened. Poor old Gilly. Bad karma.

Probably already feeling like he should be on 701 already, Warnie continued plugging away and it was only a matter of time. Then, he struck. Andrew Strauss, possibly deluding himself that the worm had turned for him, went for an expansive drive and was bowled.

Unlike Monty's first Ashes wicket in Perth, there was no tangible delay; there was a huge outpouring of noise. Up went the crowd, and off went Warnie, on an almost Monty-esque circuit of the square, one arm raised aloft in the style of Mary Poppins himself, Alan Shearer. Whether you wanted to enjoy it or not, it was a 'hairs on the back of the neck' moment. I had more of these thanks to having binoculars instead of clippers.

The din continued for a few seconds and then the entire crowd stood as one to acclaim this superb achievement. Warne is a flamboyant character but seems to have a sense of humility about him when acknowledging his fans and the applause. That kind of phlegmatic approach 'man in the street' persona does him great credit.

It was nice to see that he got a wicket using a classic mode of dismissal, against a recognised batsman, on his home ground, on the big cricket day of the year, against his favourite opponents and on a public holiday, perfect. And Adam Gilchirst wasn't involved.

It was a 'Roy of the Rovers' style moment, and makes you wonder if the Roy Race's cricket equivalent is in fact, 'Shane of St. Kilda'. The ovation was sustained, heartfelt and wholly appropriate. My bet had now gone tits up, but that was going to happen. It was good that it had occurred in this way. And now even I could be a little proud to say 'I was there'.

Those Jaegybombs must be making me soft.

Now we've got that out of the way, England had a game to win. Or lose. In each of the last three Tests they had shown heart, application and no small level of ability in defeat, but today the batting collapse was a meek surrender. The inevitable capitulation ensued and we were in a crap and almost certainly match losing position again. Our total of 159 was shoddy at best; nine boundaries told its own story.

Of course when the Aussies started to bat it all looked different as they positively raced to a trademark 40-odd for none off eight overs. The only thing to do was to find a different form of entertainment. I gave my new Tasmanian mate the old 'it was great to be here to see the second best spinner in the world get his 700th wicket' line. This was like the moment in *American Werewolf in London* when the Yanks walk into the pub and everything and everyone stops. Silence seemingly descended and for the first time I realised that Victorians had bionic hearing. Incredulity reigned.

'SECOND?!' said loads of people. I reassured them that Murali was better and the charade was played out in a wholly predictable manner:

Victoria: The Garden State

Ausse Number 1: He's a Chucker
ME: Warne's a drugs cheat.
Aussie Number 2: He's a chucker
ME: Murali only gets no-balled in Oz, by Darrel Hair
Aussie Number 3: He's a chucker

Ad infinitum.

Proving that sarcasm can exist in Australia, one of my Tassie mate's mates was helpfully commentating on the game for me. When the Aussies blazed yet another boundary he helpfully informed me in a barbed manner "That's a four". Thanks.

Chris and I had decided that we were going to make our own entertainment by having a few side bets on the action. One of the slightly unlikely bets I had today was $5 at 20-1 with him on an English bowler getting a hat-trick in the first innings. 20,000-1 looked more realistic as we toiled with the ball.

Just as you thought that it was all hopeless and the game was pretty much up, which in itself is depressing as hell before the end of a rain-shortened Day One, a breakthrough. Suddenly, out of the blue and just before close Freddie got Langer out, caught behind by Chris Read. At this point it was obvious that many of the home fans had bailed, as it was the England supporters making all the noise. Somewhat cautiously, the Australians sent out Brett Lee as night watchman.

Amazingly, he was caught behind as well, first ball, and the hat-trick was on. This was looking like THE most satisfying gambling victory of my life. Next to the crease was pesky Ricky Ponting. He was greeted with a chorus of boos as even more Aussies had now left and the visiting supporters dominated the scene. I just had enough time to say "Was that.....a wicket?" to my earlier commentator, as the cheers begin to acclaim the start of Freddie's run up. COME ON FREDDIE.

Of course it didn't happen. Ponting kept him out and the excitement was complete for a while. Strewth, close mate, but no blahddy cigaaar. Australia reached the close unscathed.

Getting into the local flavour of stating the obvious, it seems like England need to make some serious inroads in the morning session, to have any chances to win.

27 December – Day 2 Melbourne Test
England 159
Australia 372-7

I had a bit of a chuckle with Chris this morning as despite it being largely cloudy and gloomy yesterday, he'd managed to burn his head. My St George cross bandana has been like a godsend to me, despite the fact that it has helped people single me out for abuse and probably looked a bit shit.

The first hour today was superb with England making a real fist of it. I'm a little ashamed to admit I was late again, waiting for my mate to change his flights, but this guilt turned to joy as we heard a massive cheer as we made our way around the ground. As a fan of sport, you are able to train your ears to know exactly what is going on. This cheer could be only one of two things. Either someone had hit the ball out of the MCG (virtually impossible) or it was a wicket. Within a few seconds we had the confirmation, once again I'd missed Ponting getting out, but that didn't matter, Freddie had struck again, and it really was game on. The England players were totally effervescent in the field now. They had the Aussies on the run and just maybe the pressure was off a little bit. The Ashes had gone and there was pride to play for. Historically, England have done well in these situations. This probably explains why we have only lost 5-0 in Australia once before.

Victoria: The Garden State

In this series, getting Ponting out has been really tough, and getting rid of the seemingly impregnable Hussey has been a nightmare. With such a modest total on the board, we had to get him early. His scores so far in the series had been 86, 91, 61 not out, 74 not out and 103. A handy average of around 140. Mr Cricket indeed.

All this made the fact that Hoggard bowled him for just six even more appetising.

As Flintoff had gone off the field for a moment after drinks, Andrew Strauss took the reins and his first act was to throw the ball to Harmison. With his second ball he got the edge of Clarke's bat, Read took his third catch and suddenly the Australians were 84-5 and reeling. And now came the Birmingham-born Symonds.

He was greeted with the kind of passage of play that Test cricket is all about. Symonds is undoubtedly an aggressive batsman, a clean hitter who looks more confident when he is playing freely. What followed was some excellent bowling from Harmison, Hoggard and Mahmood and this belligerent player was totally becalmed. Eventually it took him 20 balls to get off the mark and he looked all over the shop. At lunch the score was 108-5 and the game still very much in the balance.

By tea it was totally imbalanced.

Hayden and Symonds (they are great mates apparently) batted all the way through the afternoon session. This was like déjà vu all over again. The game was tight and then suddenly it was totally one-sided. The questions were simple, are the Aussies that good? Are we that bad? As ever, probably a bit of both. Anyway, during the afternoon I'd had enough of sitting sedately and so went to join a standing section behind the Barmy Army seats. The standing section was weird; it was like a little platform, or even a stage, just peeking out from under the stand, with room for about 75 at a push. You had a letterbox view of the action and a regular chant of *My Garden*

Shed Is Bigger Than This was struck up. As Hayden and Symonds milked the runs, the cricket seemed largely irrelevant. In the end a letterbox view was too much, maybe I should have brought my binoculars and employed them the wrong way around.

So in the end I just stayed there all day, sinking lagers at a steady rate and enjoying the banter. As usual this was generally one-sided, with the more tuneful and inventive England fans holding sway, despite staring down the barrel of a 4-0 score line.

Then came the best chant of the tour so far. Now I'm no major royalist by any means (although I've always found German people charming, especially in Germany) but it's one sure fire way of goading the Aussies. So to the tune of *Convict Colony* (maybe that should be *Yellow Submarine*), all together now

Your next Queen is Camilla Parker Bowles, Camilla Parker Bowles, Camilla Parker Bowles.

It would serve them right if it was, and if she won their beloved Melbourne Cup. As an owner obviously, not as a runner. Hell no.

Everyone laughed at this song.

Back on the field and Andrew Symonds got a very important century, probably cementing his place in the side for a while. He proper did his nut afterwards, perhaps to reinforce his Aussie credentials. Sadly, he can do the Aussie accent quite well. It'd be loads more fun if he'd stayed Brummie and run down the wicket to his team mate Hayden and said "Oiv dun it Hoiders, oiv got mi tun. Shuddup Koy Poy, you Saath African bastid." Let's imagine he did anyway.

Finally, 64 overs and 279 runs after they came together, the partnership was broken. Saj Mahmood got Hayden, and then quickly removed fan's favourite Adam 'Gilly' Gilchrist, and this gave us a chance to serenade Shane Warne for one of the final times. Just because this was his 700 party, he was in no way spared. The

Warne song for this series, again to the versatile tune of *My Old Man's a Dustman* has been:

> Shane Warne is an Aussie, He likes to play around
> He's got a different girlfriend, in every cricket town
> He's always into trouble, he's always into strife
> And when he lost his hair, HE ALSO LOST HIS WIFE.

It was sung with a great gusto, a true back-handed compliment to the man.

My thirsty guzzling had left me a little tipsy once again, so it was time to crash out for the day. This match was totally lost and the cricket was becoming an irrelevance and an embarrassment in equal measures.

Maybe it had been all along, but the big 5-0 was definitely on the cards now.

28 December – Day 3 Melbourne Test
England 159 & 161
Australia 419
Australia won by an innings and 99 runs

The Brisbane and Perth Tests looked unlikely to make it to five days and managed to get there. This one never looked like going beyond four, and in the end we got an extra day holiday. Well done to the England players for such an inept display. Maybe that's harsh, but from my garden shed, that's how it looked to me.

The day started in relatively inauspicious circumstances as I went to get my haircut. A bloke in an adjacent chair heckled me about England. Fair play to the Aussies, the geezer felt like he could climb into me even though he had silver foil and bleach on his head. "You having your highlights done there mate?" I felt duty bound to ask. He shut up then.

All the papers are full of England's bowling plans for each of the Aussie batsmen being leaked. This is meat and drink to the media, a classic opportunity to kick someone when they are down. Presumably the concept of individualised plans for each batsman is pretty normal in the modern game and if it was England 4-0 up after four in Australia (please please one day please), this would be a non-story. Now it just gives everyone a chance to pillory England further.

It's quite an interesting read really. The highlights for me are 'Throat bouncer (surprise)' for Warnie, that's a nice touch. The other one is the suggestion that if you bowl him enough dot balls, Matthew Hayden's ego will get the better of him. Apparently this was read out on air during the mammoth Hayden/Symonds partnership. You can imagine the guffawing on the radio as this was done. The problem England have is that they can't win in this, and if they had no plan they'd be getting panned.

Making my way to the ground today, there seemed little point in going to my seat, so it was straight to the garden shed for a bit of a singsong. On my way round to the standing area, one of the witty Aussies laid the "Don't you wish your grandfather had nicked a loaf of bread?' line on me." I'd had this one before, so replied with "he did mate, he just wasn't stupid enough to get caught," which was OK, I'd settle for that.

Despite the hopeless match situation, the beer flowed and as I went to get my first it reminded me of my first visit to the MCG. I didn't really know what to expect food-wise at the cricket and had wondered if the Australians had barbeques or maybe ate seafood and salads and that. What I found was a surprise and then totally unsurprising at the same time. The food was quintessentially English. You could buy pies, chips and hotdogs, and that was about it. They were more obsessed with salt, vinegar and ketchup than we were. Brilliant.

Anyway, the day's cricket had a major air of inevitability about it and England were annihilated. In the other Tests, the problem was that England couldn't string two good innings together, in this one they just got battered. It was as poor as it was totally monotonous.

The day began with Australia batting but there was welcome relief when the English-born Andrew Symonds was first out, adding just two to his overnight score and falling to Steve Harmison for 156. Just three less than the entire England team. After that slow and nervous start yesterday, you had to hand it to him. When he had a spell as an overseas player with Lancashire, he seemed to be the archetypal 'shit or bust' type player. He either got a ton or got nowt. This was the day he filled his boots, and presumably the chants of "Judas, Judas" didn't bother him too much. We were then 'treated' to a cameo 40 not out by one S.K. Warne, who's batting continues to impress. Finally England got through the tail and it was time for business.

England actually started their reply well, with Strauss and Cook passing 40 for the first time in the series. Then the rain started. Unfortunately this wasn't a monsoon, which might have saved the day, but the steady drip, drip, drip of wickets. Once Cook went, the writing was on the wall in indelible ink. It looked like England were playing a different game and maybe using different equipment. We managed to muster a measly eight boundaries in the whole innings. Symonds hit 15, Hayden, you know him with the big ego, got 13. Our second knock amassed a total just two runs greater than our feeble first innings effort.

The England fans sung their hearts out but this was no longer to back the team, they were long gone, it was more about laughing in the face of adversity. This was just painful, a total landslide victory. Even the distinctly ordinary Brett Lee (I'm sticking with my views on him) managed to rustle up four wickets, so things really didn't get much worse than this.

The right team had been picked we just weren't good enough. Maybe, just maybe, if the right side had been selected from the start of the tour, things would have been different. Monty in Adelaide would have been a mouth-watering proposition. But we'd probably still have lost the series.

For the Fourth consecutive Test, it was time to have a look at the cricket through the bottom of a glass.

29 December

By far the weirdest day of the tour so far.

It felt quite strange to wake up with a pretty free schedule. I enjoyed the idea of a day off. When I'm in my 'civvies', that is, no bandana, no flag, it's not that easy to spot that I'm English. It almost felt like the only extra clothing I was wearing was a cloak of anonymity. And it felt just fine.

Today's simple task was to take the bike I hired back to the shop. Pretty simple. It was a rather hot day today and I was halfway through the short ride to the hire shop and then the chain came off. This was a bit of a pain to be honest but even someone of my poor levels of mechanical dexterity could fix it. Then it happened again and I was getting a bit of a sweat on, and pretty cacked up with oil but it was fine.

Eventually I made it back to the hire shop, only I didn't. I couldn't find it. Now this is typical me so I checked, double checked and triple checked but it just wasn't there. A week ago it was right there by the river, this really helps as a point of reference as there is really only one river going through the centre of Melbourne and even I can remember which side it was on.

Victoria: The Garden State

Trying to be logical, I went back to the Tourist Info place which gave me the bike hire address and tried to play dumb (not a problem) and asked if there was a bike hire place in the area. No they say. So I showed the lady the receipt I had, and she gave me a knowing look.

"Yeah, they've moved we think, let me show you where it is on a map." About two miles down the road. Bike ride there, bus/cab/tram back, no thanks. If the owner's reading, and he won't be, the bike is at the Mercure Hotel on Little Bourke Street, and keep the $20 deposit, it's fine honestly.

So I headed back to the aforementioned hotel and it dawned on me that last night I'd had a text to inform me that there was an outstanding voicemail on my mobile. I rang it and the news wasn't great. A job I had lined up to go home to seemed to be in jeopardy, and I needed to make some urgent phone calls to get it sorted. The problem, it was about midnight in the UK so I wouldn't be able to call, thereby giving me all day to fret about it.

I had some time to kill so I thought I'd give the old blog a bit of thought. Some of the Aussies had been laying into me a bit so I figured it would be a good time to give their team a bit of credit. I also tried to explain to the minority that most of the banter is a bit of a wind-up really, just like the England fans singing "Feed the Aussies, let them know it's Christmas time." Having been on the receiving end of that song whilst watching Everton, at Newcastle of all places, I knew how puerile it was really. Anyway, this blog was a bit of an attempt to restore a modicum of balance.

I had revelled in the abuse and banter up to this point, but this was an odd day. Later in the evening I signed on to see a succession of comments from the same bloke who was pretty much calling me a Fat C**t over and over again. Now in the eyes of the law this may not be libellous, some would say it's factually correct, but it felt peculiar to be reading this about myself.

171

Luckily this passed and a few people, both English and Aussies leapt to my defence and in the end it was quite touching. A couple of phone calls later, and just like the authorities organising the back burning, it looked as though I'd put out the fire of my job problems too.

Phew. Watching England get battered at the cricket is simpler than this.

30 December

Today's going to be a better day. The pressure is off, so I decide to have a stroll down to Federation Square, grab a paper and get myself some al fresco dining.

It's a beautiful day today, and would be perfect for a game of cricket. Sadly, English inability to last more than three days has put paid to this and also, thinking about it, to any conspiracy theories about the games being dragged on unnecessarily due to a greedy TV mogul. Melbourne looks great today. The city gloriously combines the traditional and the modern. Flinders Street Station is a traditional old building lovingly restored, dwarfed in the background by sleek steel skyscrapers, which positively glisten in the sunshine.

If it wasn't Christmas already, the Australian press would still be feeling festive as they take great pleasure in savaging the England Team, Coach and overall set-up.

The Age had the most brutal and barbed angle. The front cover featured two pictures and two statements. The first was a picture of a Day Four ticket for the forthcoming Sydney Test with the proclamation 'This may be the most useless ticket in Australia'. Lower on the page was a pic of Freddie making a sign of a gun to his head with his hand and the avowal 'And this may be the captain of the worst England team ever.'

Victoria: The Garden State

The most amazing thing about the accompanying copy is that there are several paragraphs and the term 'Poms' isn't used once. Must be a pretty highbrow paper *The Age*.

Our great British press are also steaming in and the sheer weight of former England players in the media means that there is no place to hide really. I am detecting a correlation between the age of the critics and the sheer unpleasantness of their approach. Some of the more recent retirees, probably those who have faced many of this outstanding Aussie team, seem a little more constructive in their criticism, talking about strategy and planning. The old school players refer more to heart and fight.

It's like a big game of 'pile-on' in the playground really. A bit of fun to play but ultimately unsatisfying. In yesterday's *Herald Sun*, the nightmare scenario happened and the big lad jumped on top of the pile.

Mike Gatting's criticism was pretty stinging, using words like 'crap' and 'stupid.' He also reminded us that he was good batsman and a not so good bowler with the comment. "Our poor batters go out and have nothing to defend and all to chase. It has been a disaster from day one with the bowlers." My view, for what it's worth, the batsmen had a chance to do much better in Adelaide on the last day, and they were also found wanting in Perth (when the bowlers did the business) and in the first innings in Melbourne.

The truth is they are better at fielding, batting and bowling, and you ain't going to win many games under those circumstances.

Australian coach John Buchanan, who takes po-faced to a new level, even out-douring England coach and stern king Duncan Fletcher, has been mischievously suggesting that he doesn't perceive Kevin Pietersen to be a team player. John, you've won, relax and enjoy it.

So it's the last day in Melbourne today. It's a quality and buzzing place but in all honesty caught me in a funny mood. It seems a pity that the Ashes Tour runs in this order really. It'd be great to start off in Melbourne and Sydney, the two major cities, and then make your way around the quieter ones as the energy levels start to dip. There is also talk of extending the next Aussie-hosted Ashes to six Test matches, incorporating Hobart in Tasmania, which is supposed to be beautiful.

6-0, 5-0, what's the difference really?

Tomorrow it's off to Sydney for New Year's Eve, they go proper mental over that, and a couple of non-cricket things I'd like to check out as well. If time permits, I might have a look at the Test Match too.

NEW SOUTH WALES: THE PREMIER STATE

"WHEN YOU HAVE TO KILL A MAN IT COSTS NOTHING TO BE POLITE."

WINSTON CHURCHILL
(BRITISH PRIME MINISTER)

31 December - Arrive Sydney

Goodbye Mel, hello Syd.

Having got down to the airport at a reasonable time in order to pick up my tea-time flight, there was a little commotion as an earlier flight to Sydney had been cancelled. This meant that a handful of Aussies in party gear were in danger of literally 'missing the boat' for their extravagant trips around the famous Circular Quay to mark the start of 2007.

It seemed strange to see Australians in formal gear really. There are many things to lampoon about this country, and in loads of ways for a supposedly laid back place they seem pretty regimented, but many informalities are to be applauded. Again it's linked to the climate, but if you try to get into a decent bar in the UK wearing shorts, whether its 100 degrees or not, you are very likely to attract the damning 'not tonight lads' from Norman the Doorman.

Not so here. At least this plane touched down on time to give all revellers a sporting chance.

Also, and maybe you like it, but I HATE being called 'Sir.' Over here, everybody uses the word 'mate' and this is to be applauded. Puts you right at ease.

Anyway, it's party-time for the Sydneysiders and the millions of visitors, yet for your average Australian cricket journalist, Christmas just never stops. Operating under the widely held assumption that the Test Series will end 5-0, the hacks are now turning their poison pens towards England's one-day form. It's hard to argue with this angle really, our one-day performance has been rubbish for years and it has seemed for a long time that the management team, probably quite rightly, have placed for more emphasis on the Test side. Having watched the England players in Melbourne visibly wilt under the force of the Aussies, the Tri-Nations series is not a pleasant prospect. At least I won't be there to see that particular landslide.

Despite the fact that England seem to be the 'Kings of the Dead Rubber' when it comes to Ashes Tests, and this also tends to be true of the Rugby League too, the Aussies seem hell-bent on doing all they can to expunge their 2005 Ashes defeat from the records. Since Adelaide, 5-0 has been very much a possibility. and with his final Test coming up, Glenn McGrath must be pissing himself. Not laughing, just pissing himself.

Also in the news are reports of a bit of sledging between Andrew Symonds and Kevin Pietersen during the Melbourne Test. Apparently this started when KP accused the English-born Australian all-rounder of being in the side as a specialist fielder. Symonds response was to suggest that Pietersen's luggage wouldn't weigh much, as he goes out wearing singlets (vests to you and me). Seems a little bit juvenile really and not up there with Eddo Brandes' "Every time I fuck your missus she gives me a biscuit" or timeless classics like that.

New South Wales: The Premier State

Sadly for England and KP, and typical of how things have gone so far this tour, it's being alleged that the criticism stung Symonds into action and inspired him to his century in the Boxing Day Test. This all seems pretty unlikely as a) he looked really dodgy at the start of his innings b) if that was all it took to get him to a century, his team-mates would have been saying it ages ago.

Back to the forthcoming final Test and it is clear that England's best chance of stopping the whitewash and to rain on the Aussies' parade - is for it to rain on the Aussies' parade. The weather forecast is pretty dodgy for the coming week. I can envisage a situation whereby the Australians make some kind of aggressive declaration as time is running out and leave England with a gettable target, and England just go and get them. 4-1. A defeat in the Final Test of Warne, McGrath and countless others perhaps. A moral victory, and mouth-watering morsel from the mighty Aussie table.

Elsewhere, Muralitharan has intimated that he will tour Australia again, despite the fact that he gets no-balled and pilloried wherever he plays. His crime? Chucking or maybe simply not being Shane Warne. The choice is yours. If the great Murali actually makes the trip, the fascinating possibility arises that he may break Warne's Test wickets world record in Australia. Sweet.

No doubt Darrel Hair is dusting down his white shirt and black keks as we speak, hoping for the chance to nail him in some warm-up match.

By the time I made it to Sydney, the New Year celebrations were starting to warm up, but I was heading in the opposite direction from the crowds to go and stay at my mate Chris' hotel for a couple of nights. Not that he owns a hotel, but he does have a room in one, and finding somewhere decent to stay on New Year's Eve in Sydney is not the easiest task. So he's kindly agreed that he'll make his room into a twin for a couple of nights for a mere 50% of the overall cost.

Ashes To Dust

The hotel is in the King's Cross area of Sydney, one of the most vibrant parts of the city, a kind of Soho before the facelift type environment. Apparently it's cleaned itself up quite a lot in recent times, but it still has a seedy feel that is not completely unappealing. This place is buzzing all year round anyway, but on New Year's Eve was absolutely heaving.

We headed down to Circular Quay to try to get a view of the Harbour Bridge and the first thing to notice is just how damned organised the whole Sydney New Year's Eve thing is. There are loads of police around, but in fairness they all seem pretty mellow and are wholly disinterested in people boozing in the street, they just seemed keen to keep any real idiots in check. Maybe they are on the look out for proper criminals, ones who carry inflatable crocodiles or perhaps even trumpets.

It's always been a funny old night New Year's Eve, one of those occasions back home where you often feel under pressure to do something that's really 'out there', but the excesses of Christmas make you feel like doing the exact opposite. What helps here is that at least it's pretty warm, so there's no need to get the 'hot ticket' for a bar or club, because there are zillions of people out and about anyway.

By the time midnight approached, there was plenty of broken glass and stuff around, and everyone seemed to have at least one camera each (some seemingly more) to catch some grainy footage of the fireworks that greeted 2007. It's easy to be cynical (about everything), but fireworks are just a little bit too common these days. When you spent the whole year waiting for the effects of an 'Air Bomb Repeater' or the 'Screecher', you know, the one from the Supersonic Six, it was really something. Now it seems like, New Year – fireworks, Chinese New Year – fireworks, Christmas – fireworks, Bonfire Night – effigy burning followed by fireworks. The Sydney display was all well and groovy and after hours of anticipation, a few minutes and no doubt oodles of dollars worth of pyrotechnics, it was all over.

There was a pleasant atmosphere once the New Year had begun as people trudged their way through the debris and made their way to the next destination. This reminded me of a story I was told by a lad who went to New York for New Year and plodded through Times Square in the early hours of the morning. Apparently the area was strewn with used adult nappies, employed by the revellers so they could maintain their place. I have done nothing to corroborate this story, but it'd be nice to believe.

Obviously, this is oft repeated by me as an example of the obscenity of American life, with one fatal error. I always, for some unknown reason, say 'human' nappies instead of adult, which just doesn't sound the same. Until the realisation dawns on me, I always feel slightly cheated by the lack of shock and awe (another American thang) on the face of the unsuspecting victim for the story.

As we headed back to King's Cross, which is pretty much a 24-hour suburb anyway and maybe was just getting started, it was time to turn in. Tomorrow is the eve of the Fifth Test and we've got to head out to Coogee to grab the tickets.

1 January

The seemingly simple task of picking up the tickets was a little trickier than first thought.

The day started well in the sense that it was nice to phone home and another positive, it was raining really quite hard. It's a pretty sad indictment of confidence levels in the England Team, but this was what we'd been reduced to really, relying on inclement weather in a country which has sunshine just about everyday and a big hole in the ozone layer just above it.

179

Then it was off to organise the Coogee coup, a couple of bus rides to a beachside suburb a few miles outside the centre of Sydney.

The event at the Coogee Oval was the next of seemingly hundreds of cricket matches between The Fanatics and The Barmy Army. I must admit to not really having followed the other games avidly, but I was left with the lasting impression that the Aussies were cleaning up. It was heartening if a little unnerving to see 11 Fanatics in the same place at the same time, good effort lads.

I found it hard not to reflect on the folly of paying way over the odds for tickets to the fifth Test. Back in the late summer of 2006 in the UK, I was really excited when I found out tickets were available and remember thinking about how things might pan out. This could be the chance to see the final confirmation of the changing of the guard; the youthful exuberance of the vibrant young England Team, retaining the Ashes at the SCG and damning half the Aussie side to retirement at the same time. It really was a case of what might have been. In reality it was always going to be a bit of a struggle, but 4-0 with one to play was still hard to believe and even tougher to stomach.

As we arrived at the Oval it was clear that this wasn't going to be any kind of smash and grab raid. Typically after the morning deluge, the sun was shining brightly now, and it was a characteristically hot Aussie summer's day. Sadly the ticket queue was moving at a rate that would make a one-lunged snail look like Ben Johnson at the Seoul Olympics. The conditions were a grave contrast from those experienced by lucky punters waiting in the rain at Melbourne on Christmas Day, but it was still hard work, melting in the heat.

The cricket match was brought to life by a streaker, who was accosted and covered, using a St. George cross, by non-other than the Barmy Army's Jimmy. The 'he's only got one song' chant could easily be extended to 'he's only got one outfit.' The sleeveless St. George cross T-shirt and white jeans ensemble is as recognisable as his perma-tan and seemingly indefatigable ability to drink, sing and watch cricket. I have nothing but admiration for anyone who can wear white strides and still retain a modicum of dignity; for us lesser mortals they just seem like an accident waiting to happen. He makes it look so easy.

After seemingly hours, but probably only an hour, and a horrible rumour near the front of the queue we would only get Day One tickets, I finally had my grubby mits on the tickets for the Fifth and Final Test.

It seems an appropriate time to thank Cricket Australia for just how difficult they have made this process. I sincerely commend them on how much money they have contributed to the grey/black economy, with E-bay sharks, corporate ticket agencies and ticket touts in both the UK and Australia making a killing. Thanks a million.

Looking forward to tomorrow, another Aussie bites the dust as Justin Langer has decided to call it a day as well. It is often said that the really great batsmen are below average height, but probably not so short. Five foot Justin, the man even Ricky Ponting calls Stumpy, has again fallen straight into England's intricate trap. Our strategy to lose 5-0 and sucker all the Australian stalwarts into retiring has been carried out with clinical efficiency. Adelaide was just a ruse to give the Australians that awestruck feeling that they'd pulled off some memorable victory, just to finish things off in style. And ensuring Warne went to Melbourne on 699 wickets was a masterstroke. Don't you just love it when a plan comes together?

Of course we may not lose 5-0 at all. There is talk that England may field two spinners for the last Test. The last time we did this here the pair in question were would-be triathletes Phil Tufnell and Eddie Hemmings, and they picked up 12 wickets as England bagged a draw. That'd do.

This time the twirlers in tandem would be Monty and the recently arrived Jamie Dalrymple. He's arrived in the place of Ashley Giles, who has had to return home to care for his sick wife.

With Glenn McGrath, Martin O'Neill, Darren Clarke and many, many more, it does seem strange that so many famous sporting figures have wives suffering from serious illnesses, and makes you wonder whether there is any connection between the stressful lifestyle, days away from home and so on.

Think I'll leave it there.

Pleasingly the weather forecast for tomorrow and the next few days is now much better. Brilliant.

2 January - Day 1 Sydney Test
England 234-4

Slate grey skies were the order of the day, with the prospect of any play looking pretty bleak as day broke over the impressive Sydney skyline.

Despite having been over here for six weeks now, it is hard to get used to just how quickly the weather can change. When you've watched most of your cricket in Blackpool, Manchester and more latterly Leeds, if it's raining in the morning then you are not going to get amazing odds on it raining in the afternoon and evening too. Here, if it's raining, you may as well get sorted and down to the ground because play is likely to start pretty promptly.

As it goes, play was delayed by just 40 minutes and the news was that England had won the toss, decided to bat and that Jimmy Anderson had been called up in place of Hoggard, who was injured. This was a bit disappointing, but seemed somewhat trivial in the grand scheme of things. Today was all about Warne, McGrath and to a lesser extent (not just because of his height) Justin Langer.

The fielding side came out to a tremendous ovation and it was noticeable that there were painted tributes daubed on the out-field by the sponsors 3 mobile, with the words 'Thx Shane, Thx

Justin and Thx Glenn,' which was a nice touch and a pretty handy bit of marketing really. It does seem a little incongruous that the Test Series is sponsored by 3 mobile while loads of the Aussies seem to be carrying first generation mobiles with them, but maybe that's the point.

Our view in the ground was excellent, high up in a stand in one of the more 'civilised' areas of the SCG, and immediately I was disappointed. I would have preferred to be situated right in the thick of the England Barmy Army support, but vowed to myself that I'd get down there and get involved later. The SCG seems to be a ground that is loved by the locals, but on both of my visits it's seemed like a bit of a dump to me; a kind of hotch-potch of different stands and no real areas for supporters to congregate.

As the action started, it was clear that despite being away from the cheap seats I was within earshot of one of the loudest cricket fans on the planet. In fact, within earshot is wrong. People at the top of the Sydney Harbour Bridge were within earshot, I just had the misfortune of being pretty near him as well. After McGrath had made his way in and gingerly delivered a harmless first ball of the match, this Aussie, a big geezer probably in his late 30s, delivered his first, booming "Well bowled Glenn". Fair enough. Sadly this followed every subsequent delivery of the over. He may have varied it with the occasional "Bowling Ooh-Ah" (as in Ooh-Ah Glenn McGrath), but he definitely had something to say every ball. I tried to make allowances for this ear-splitting behaviour, maybe the lad was excited and it was McGrath's last Test after all. Not a bit of it.

Brett Lee got the same and the die was cast for the day. Then our fan, let's call him Bruce for the sake of argument, achieved something that I have never seen before or even considered possible. There is a slightly lame but well-established practice at sporting events for fans to compel their heroes to 'give them a wave'. It usually starts with a handful singing it, and then hundreds join in and tend to achieve around a 50% success rate, contributory factors are the state of the game, the individual who should be waving and the general background noise.

Well, our Bruce managed it on his own. Three times. Hussey, Clarke and Langer all provided the requisite hand gesture, as Bruce's compelling, deafening tones demanded it. This man made Brian Blessed sound like Orville the Duck, honestly. His dander (whatever that is) well and truly up, he then went for Billy Bowden, who was stood at square leg, probably about 60 yards away. You could see the flamboyant Kiwi umpire seriously consider the request, he flinched using a gesticulation not dissimilar to his nose scratching motion, which fooled me at Brisbane, but didn't go for a full wave in the end. And our Bruce seemed genuinely surprised and disappointed.

Back on the pitch, England got through the first half of the session unscathed; although Strauss was spared as Langer marked his Final Test with a dropped catch.

THX JUSTN U LTL FCKR.

As ever with England and particular the openers, their luck didn't hold for long and Strauss was out with the score at 45. Yet again, they had got a start but not been able to go on. Damn! Cook quickly followed and it looked like Melbourne all over again until a significant partnership between two players who had come in for a lot of stick from the Aussie press and players.

It was time for Ian Bell (looks like someone out of a film) and Kevin Pietersen (South African, selfish, wears vests, would make a great Aussie) to show some real grit and determination and get England back on track. Pietersen in particular was showing some seriously aggressive intent, audaciously dancing down the pitch to Glenn McGrath, the ultimate insult for the legendary fast bowler in his final Test. And the ploy was working as the England pair amassed a century partnership. There is no doubt that McGrath has lost pace as time has caught up with him, but he couldn't have expected this. As one English wit near me remarked: "It's nice to see KP coming down the track to the spinners." If only we could have got Bruce to repeat that, McGrath would have been fuming.

The atmosphere in the ground built nicely, with one group of about 200 Aussies amassed near the Barmy Army all wearing the same garish yellow T-shirts. This could have been one of the world's biggest Stag trips as surely that is the only example of when it is socially accepted to all wear the same clobber. Maybe Australia has a stupidly high divorce rate, thereby explaining why so many of them have to wear the same stuff all the time. Or perhaps they are just sad.

Anyway this group 'treated' the crowd to a rendition of *Advance Australia Fair* and some kind of new song they'd dreamt up with a last line of "All Pommies are Wankers." As usual, the sound of fingernails being scraped slowly down a blackboard would have been infinitely more pleasing on the ear than this din. I'd rather we were good at cricket than singing to be honest, but some of the Aussie fans do take charmlessness to an entirely new level.

Back to the action, and as Sod's Law would have it, McGrath found a way of eeking out both England batsmen and once again the game was in the balance, especially as this England side has a tail longer than a long-tailed possum.

The clatter of wickets brought Flintoff and Collingwood together and for the first time in the series, Freddie started to show some real form with the bat. He looked really calm and assured as he approached a half-century. In fact, England scored at a decent pace towards the end of the day, with a 50 partnership being brought up in the final hour. As Chris and I had continued our Melbourne habit of betting on the events on the pitch, this gave me a problem, as my prediction of total runs in the final session was looking woefully short. As the clouds rolled to signal the approach of close of play, England were just one short of my under-egged figure, anything higher and I was a loser.

Then, finally, after six weeks in this hell-hole, something good happened. The England batsmen were offered the light and marched off purposefully, no doubt happy to have got to the end of Day One with honours even. Perhaps my gloating had reached antipodean levels, but this seemed like a lucky escape for me. My companion, however, was having none of it. The lack of small print for our bets proved to be a problem, as we disagreed somewhat on the terms of the bet. So as the patrons made their way slowly out of the SCG - and it is a nightmare to get out of - we continued to argue the toss about the bet.

So another source of in-game entertainment was in jeopardy, might have to just sit and watch the cricket tomorrow.

D'oh. England really need to be batting at lunchtime.

3 January - Day 2 Sydney Test
England 291
Australia 188-4

The banners bedecking George Street, one of the main thorough-fares in Sydney's city centre, bear the slogan 'This is our city in the summer.' Well for a large part of a mostly gloomy day it really didn't feel that way at all.

It was a strange old morning all round today, not helped by the most curious start time in the history of cricket. Yes, today play started at 10:19. Trains arrive at 10:19, cricket matches do not start at 10:19, but this one did. Because of the time lost to rain yesterday, some bright spark had come up with this time. Typically, England made a slow start to the day's play with the arrival of Freddie Flintoff's half-century being hastily followed by

Collingwood's wicket. Now the pressure was really on the England captain, mainly because the fragility of England's lower order had been proved conclusively during this series.

The Collingwood dismissal brought Chris Read to the wicket and after he made a sketchy start there followed a couple of minutes that represented a classic microcosm of the entire series. Brett Lee was steaming in to bowl to Read and when the ball struck him on the pad there was a massive appeal from the Weet-Bix Kid Lee, typically well supported by the entire fielding side. The Aussies don't so much appeal as virtually sprint over to the scoreboard to add another wicket on as they implored the umpire to give them what they see as their just deserts. The looks of incredulity on their faces if the match officials don't give them what they expect, are akin to that weird face Neil Warnock pulls when someone has the temerity to give a decision against his beloved Blades.

Unusually in this series, and yes that is a whinge, the umpire held his nerve and turned down the appeal. So wrapped up in their histrionics were the Aussie team that they forgot the ball, and Flintoff and Read scampered two runs, even though the ball had hardly left the square.

This was pure comedy and the Englishmen in the crowd, making up around 50% of those in attendance, collectively chuckled at the expense of the hosts. Fantastic.

The laughter had barely subsided when Lee got Read out next ball. And then Mahmood was out off the very next delivery. Bloody typical.

Flintoff, now knowing full well that he had very little left to bat with, decided to hit out and was eventually out for 89, his best score of the series, and received an excellent reception from the crowd. He apparently got a lot of credit here for his sportsmanship during the 2005 Ashes Series, and there seemed like a genuine sense of warmth for him. It also looked like there was some genuine admiration for this colossus who'd always given 100% in a losing cause, irrespective of any shortcoming he may or may not have as captain.

England's innings petered out in trademark fashion and the only other item of note was that Justin Langer dropped two more catches.

THX AGAIN SHRTY.

So once again it was time for the England bowlers to have a go at defending what looked like a sub-standard first innings total. The Aussies set off in their typically brutal fashion, punishing any minor errors from the opening Lancashire pair of Anderson and Flintoff. Jimmy looks the part as an opening bowler and it's nice to see him fulfilling the role he clearly prefers, rather than a bit-part player grazing in the outfield all day. He picked up Langer's wicket - not having the best of final games our Justin - but the Australians in the formidable form of Hayden and Ponting took charge in a wholly predictable way.

The home side were making their way relentlessly forward, despite the loss of Hayden, and had 118 on the board when an apparently pivotal moment occurred. The pesky but quite honestly brilliant Ponting was batting with his mate Mike Hussey and we had all seen far too much of these two to know that it was ominous for England. Then it happened. Ponting hit the ball to Jimmy Anderson at mid-on and set off for a sharp single. Jimmy picked up and unleashed a great throw to hit the stumps and this one looked really, really close. Once again the number of people with radios played a major part as the buzz around the ground quickly imparted the news that Ponting was out. A throaty chant of "Cheerio, Cheerio, Cheerio" reverberated around the SCG as Ponting awaited confirmation from the big screen. As sure as jockeys should be put down if their horses have to be, the word 'OUT' appeared and Ricky was on his way. With the Aussies at 118-3, England were right in the game.

New South Wales: The Premier State

After a short partnership between Hussey and Clarke, Harmison got his second wicket of the innings and now it was time for the English-born Andrew Symonds. Unfortunately, he only got halfway to the wicket when the rain came pouring down. To be honest, he looked a proper clown having to get half way out there and then turn back. This was more to do with his lipstick and hair combo rather than the situation, though.

Having been craving rain for a couple of weeks now to stop the whitewash, this interlude seemed a little unwelcome as England were in a decent position. In fact, the game was superbly poised. What followed was a familiar scene with plenty of home fans taking the opportunity to slope off home, whilst the fervent away supporters hung around in the vain hope that there would be play.

With this being Australia, after 90 minutes or so the players were back out there, with about half an hour to play in the dazzling evening sunshine. I took the opportunity to sneak over to join the slightly depleted ranks of the Barmy Army. There was a great moment when Monty performed a pretty competent piece of fielding slap bang in front of the England fans. This got a cheer almost to compare with the one to greet Ponting's dismissal earlier.

Monty was coolness personified as he jogged back into position, beseeching the Barmy Army for further noise and adulation, as the rays of the setting sun seemed to form a halo around him. Great that. It's paradoxical that one of the fears about Monty was that he would get a gruesome reaction from the Australian support, yet at this moment he didn't seem to have a care in the world. Untainted by the disaster at Adelaide, and outstanding with bat and ball in the first half of the Perth Test, Panesar had arrived. And his fielding was coming on in leaps and bounds too. Hopefully he could bowl England to victory in this game just to finish things off nicely.

My own trip to Australia was also finishing off nicely and things had, thankfully, definitely calmed down on the boozing front.

Sydney is a really vibrant city and there's loads going on. Just walking the streets in the early evenings is a very pleasant experience and the cosmopolitan nature of the place is wholly apparent. My new hotel described itself as a 'boutique hotel', which I sadly misinterpreted as meaning 'really smart, very modern and a little bit quirky.' What it really meant was no cable TV and definitely no internet access.

So it was a good job that pounding the Sydney streets was fascinating, because seeking out internet cafés was once again part of my daily routine. My blog wasn't going to write itself and it was important to give my 'adoring' Aussie public an outlet for their endless stream of abuse.

4 January - Day 3 Sydney Test
England 291 & 114-5
Australia 393

On the walk down to the station to get a shuttle bus to the SCG, it really felt like a case of déjà vu all over again as England needed early breakthroughs to force home a reasonable position. They have had chances to ram home advantageous situations in the past three Tests and just not managed it; perhaps today would be different. After all, we were due a change of luck.

The atmosphere was quite relaxed in the SCG, with probably 50% of those in attendance supporting the away team once again. The day started brilliantly with Hussey going early, and after a troublesome partnership between Symonds and Gilchrist, our hero Monty, removed the English-born all-rounder to give England a whiff of success. What followed was likely to decide the game. If England could knock over the Australian tail, we were looking at a first innings lead and a pretty strong chance of winning the Test.

New South Wales: The Premier State

What ensued was actually some of the most compelling cricket of the entire tour. Warne strode to the wicket with the gait of a gunslinger, and was greeted with the customary rousing reception. This was his last ever Test, and whatever you thought of him, cricket would not be the same after he had gone. Probably the only thing missing from Shane's incomparable cricketing CV was a Test century. This could be his last chance.

Monty prowled around waiting for the applause to die down and displayed the excitement of a small child, still buzzing from getting a wicket with the first ball of this over. He bowled and somehow Warne connected with a bottom edge, and the Aussies in the crowd whooped as the ball went for four. This was something of a moral victory for the bowler, so Monty was on his toes ready to go again. Warne treated this delivery with total disdain, striding forward imperiously and swinging it for six. Warne blocked the next one, was beaten trying to smash the fifth ball of the over and then survived a huge appeal off the last. Gripping stuff.

Five overs later and the game had really started to drift away from England. The Aussies had added another 30-odd and Warne, in particular, was running amok. There were various theories being proffered as to why he should be in such a hurry: -

1. He had just a lit a cigarette
2. His pizza was going cold
3. He was on the phone to an Indian bookie when he came in and it was on his phone bill
4. He was expecting a very important text

Just as the game seemed to be up, bad karma struck Adam 'Gilly' Gilchrist as he was given out to a shocking decision. Boos rang out around the SCG, but there was nothing but cheers where I was standing. Then it occurred to me, a rare moment of clarity.

As the befuddled Gilchrist walked off there was something about his appearance that struck a real chord. On the previous evening I'd been watching footage of yet another Australian Ashes win, this time at Egbaston, probably in 2001. One of the English bowlers getting smashed around was paceman Andy Caddick, who apart from being good at cricket also shares another thing with Adam Gilchrist, somewhat curious ears.

Then I got it. They've got each others' ears. So when Gilchrist came over to cup his ears to the England fans in Perth he wasn't saying, "Cop a load of that you Pommie bastard'" what he was actually saying was "Aw Jeez look, I know it ain't the best toime for you fellas roight now but I've got your bloke's ears."

It all makes sense now. If they could swap back they'd look perfectly normal, well Caddick would anyway.

By lunch the game was nearly up, Australia already had a handy lead and we still had the thorny problem of removing Warne. There was a slight lull after lunch and then he cut loose again. The possibility of seeing Shane Warne hit his maiden Test century in his last ever Test match was becoming more and more realistic. This was too much to take. The Aussies in the crowd were going crazy and in a sense this could have been an even bigger 'I was there' moment than his 700th on Boxing Day.

As he hit three fours in one Monty over, and reached 70 off just 61 balls, it looked definitely on. Then, luckily for England, Clark got himself out so this just left the hapless (batting-wise anyway) McGrath to support Warne. This proved all too much for Warnie, as he danced down the track one more time to Panesar and was stumped. The wave of relief around the ground was tangible. Yes we were almost certainly going to see England lose 5-0, but at least we hadn't had to stomach a Warne ton.

Technically speaking the game wasn't entirely up for England, they trailed by 102 on first innings, so a good start and who knows? The problem was that they were playing the best side in the world, who were determined to mercilessly rub our noses right in it. If the roles had been reversed, you could envisage the Aussies turning this around and going on to win the game. It just wasn't going to happen.

England's reply started poorly with Cook going cheaply and then a sickening incident. Strauss ducked into a short ball from Lee, who was steaming in at over 90mph by this stage, and the stomach-churning 'thwack' on his head was all too audible. Strauss went down like the proverbial sack of spuds and it looked pretty serious for a minute. For all their rampant professionalism, the Aussie players were straight over to check on him. This showed that they do have a heart under their cold, ruthless veneer, but in all honesty also served to illustrate the seriousness of the blow he took.

My thoughts turned to the Bodyline series and just what it must have been like to hear a crack like that on someone's skull rather on a protective helmet as Harold Larwood roughed up yet another Aussie batsman. Gruesome. You had to feel for Strauss who had ended the summer in England as a possible Ashes captain and was now probably struggling just to hold his place in the side. He bravely dusted himself down and got on with it. Somewhat inevitably, he was out soon after, and the procession continued with England finishing the day five wickets down.

All that was left was to come back tomorrow and see the last rites. Fat ladies, all over Australia, were ready for a massive sing-song.

5 January - Day 4 Sydney Test
England 291 & 147
Australia 393 & 46-0
Australia won by 10 wickets
Australia wins the series 5-0

This was the 22nd and last day of Test Cricket on the tour, and still the sporting mind played tricks on me.

It stands to reason that there are more losers than winners in sport, so most of us end up being deeply pessimistic and cynical about it all. But somewhere, in the dark recesses of our minds, is that little bit of optimism that keeps us wondering. As Lord Melchett says in *Blackadder* "If nothing else works, a total pig-headed unwillingness to look facts in the face will see us through."

England were effectively 12-5 at the start of Day Four, but I still trotted along to the SCG wondering if KP could play one of those miraculous innings, like the one he played at The Oval to clinch the 2005 Ashes, and just maybe England could turn this game around and put the Aussies under pressure. Sport has a habit of messing with your mind so the dream is tantalisingly close before being snatched away at the last minute. Not so in this case.

By the time I turned up at the SCG, about five minutes after the start of play as the playing conditions had demanded yet another strange start time, I had a quick glance at the mini-scoreboard. It bore the names Read and Panesar. Bloody Pietersen was already out. So, as I assumed my position adjacent to the Barmy Army, it was now a case of just sitting through death throes of the Ashes Series.

I was sat alongside my mate Chris. We'd managed to call our bet from the other day quits, without the need to engage Butros Butros-Ghali in any peacekeeping talks. What we saw in the next few overs was a trademark England capitulation. Next to go was Monty, pushing the ball to Symonds, Australia's outstanding fielder, and being run out by a comfortable margin. After four overs of the day, England had lost two wickets and scored no runs. Very tame.

It was a gorgeous day today, clear blue skies and bright sunshine, a perfect day for a summary (or maybe that should be summery?) execution. The England fans did their best to laugh in the face of the total adversity and continued to treat the players and the rest of the crowd to a final rendition of the songs that had seen us through the past four defeats. I could understand why they would want to do this, but it served to fuel my own personal frustration. It really didn't matter that 'Symonds is a Brummie' or a Judas, or that Shane Warne had lost his hair and also lost his wife. We'd got stuffed. The ultimate indignity came when the most inane chant in sport "5-0 and you still don't sing" was unleashed on the Australian fans. Who cares? It was still 5-0. The simple fact was we had all been let down and embarrassed by the England team, and the world's greatest sing-a-long wouldn't change a thing.

As the final few wickets fell, the only question really was who would get the last one, Warne or McGrath. Warnie had enjoyed his moment of glory in Melbourne, this time it was left to McGrath to finish things off with the dismissal of Jimmy Anderson.

The two Aussie bowlers led their team off the field for the final time. Life really will be easier for England in the future without having to face these formidable opponents, but it just won't be the same. The reception those two received was heartfelt and sustained, and came from everyone in the ground.

As the England fielders formed a guard of honour for the Australian openers to take the field, my mood lifted immediately for some unknown reason. Maybe I knew the pain was about to stop. There was probably enough time before lunch for the Aussies to knock off the 40-odd runs required. As the England players got in a huddle for the last time in a Test Match on this tour, you could almost imagine Freddie saying something along the lines of 'Let's give Langer a few bruises to remember us by, but we need to be in the boozer by two o'clock at the latest.'

As it's own tribute, the Barmies treated the vertically-challenged Langer to a rendition of *Hi Ho, Hi Ho, It's Off To Work We Go* and then everybody on the field of play was implored to "Give us a Wave." This included both openers, all the England fielders and even the umpires. It was a nice moment really and kind of helped everyone get back into the 'it's only a game' sort of mindset. Everyone obliged with the one exception of Matthew Hayden. Maybe he was 'in the zone', or something.

Fittingly it was Saj Mahmood, cast in the role of superficial fifth bowler in this side, who was given the dubious privilege of sending down the final over, and then it was indeed finally over. Just about everybody hung around to hail the Aussie winners and watch the official ceremony.

The 3-mobile spokesman was treated to a chorus of "Vodafone, Vodafone, Vodafone," especially when it became apparent that he was Scottish. Everybody thanked the England fans for the fact that they had embellished the atmosphere at the games. Ricky Ponting was a little barbed in his comments, reminding us that we had not had that much to cheer about.

This was quite a poignant moment. Not because an Aussie had managed to state the obvious, I was kind of getting used to that, but for the Barmy Army this was almost full circle. Having been spawned by providing a rubbish team with excellent support, they were pretty much back to square one.

It is hard to imagine what the Aussie media and cricket fans would have made of a team on course to lose 5-0. You get the feeling that they would just not tolerate it, maybe bringing them home or even sending out a replacement team. In the 80s Australia were a pretty poor outfit, and it's hard to envisage how that would sit with their superiority complex right now. The only other thing that stood out about the ceremonials was that Ian Healy, he of the 'breast research' comment, managed to use the word 'winningest,' possibly one of THE worst American b a s t a rdisations of the English language, in referring to Aussie coach John Buchanan.

Then the players came on a lap of honour and were all warmly applauded by everyone. Matthew Hayden finally saw fit to give us all a wave, and even Adam Gilchrist managed a dignified reaction. Pleasingly, Warne, McGrath and Brett Lee, all given loads of stick by the Barmy Army, came over and milked the applause. It seems they liken the English chants to the kind of sledging they do in the middle; part of the game, done in the throes of battle and forgotten later when beer is at hand. Fair play to them.

I then spotted my mate Alan Smith, who I had chatted with in Perth, and he seemed genuinely pleased to see me and we had a bit of a natter and a photo. All was well in the world really. It was a beautiful day, we were all at a cricket match – forget the scoreline – nobody had died or even got hurt and there were far worse places to be. What's more, I was off to get drunk.

So after leaving the SCG, it was into the nearest boozer with a handful of people I had just met. I'd only really got talking to them because they had kindly warned me that my neck was getting burnt in the searing Sydney sunshine.

The atmosphere in the pub was one of a party really, there was nothing left to argue about and so everybody had a really good drink. What followed was one of the most vivid images of the tour.

After a couple of hours the pub became less rammed and some Aussie lads started playing a game of cricket, using a pool cue as a bat and some sort of softball. This took place in a kind of side-room of the pub, away from the bar and the vast majority of the punters. There were a few cheers as runs and wickets occurred in this indoor arena.

Then up stepped the mad English woman. She decided it would be a good idea to test the resolve of the Aussie batsmen by slowly pinging down the white cue ball from the pool table. This attracted a bigger crowd and a few 'oohs' and 'aahs' as she unerringly aimed for the stool that was acting as the wickets.

This only served to inspire the bowler as she began to up the pace of her deliveries. The lady in question had bright blond hair and broad shoulders, there was little doubt that the cricketer she most resembled was Brett Lee. Because of his questionable action earlier in his career, Lee had been accused of being something of a chucker. The Barmy Army had regularly treated him to choruses of *Keep Your Arm Straight When You Bowl* (to the tune of *Oh My Darling Clementine*) and shouted "No Ball" as he released the ball in his final delivery stride.

It seemed only fitting that this bowling should also be supported by the self same song, which just fired her up to strive for that extra yard of pace. Within minutes, the scenario was pretty simple, you had a drunken mad-woman, throwing a pool ball as hard as she could towards the shins of some poor unsuspecting Aussies, who had nothing but a pool cue to protect them. To make matters worse, a baying crowd was egging her on.

This is where the Aussie machismo caused them real problems. Your average Englishman would have muttered something like 'She's mental' before quickly vacating the scene. However, such is Aussie manhood that there was no shortage of volunteers to bat. To them this was all about 'sticking your hand up' or 'showing ticker'. The crowd wanted blood. These Aussie lads were putting their shins on the line as the deliveries came faster and faster.

Good sense was restored when it became apparent that the ball had been tampered with. This was no fingernail under the quarter-seam incident, though. Basically, the cue ball had hit the wall so hard that a big chunk had come out of it. Game over. Phew.

I had got chatting to some Aussie lads and the booze and banter was flowing nicely. As always, the subject of the Barmy Army came up and once again the veneration was clear to see. It seemed totally odd that the supporters of a team that had just beaten its biggest rivals 5-0 could be bothered about losing at singing. These lads completely bemoaned the state of the Aussie support.

Several drinks later I was in the Barmy Army pub in the centre of Sydney and got a call on my mobile from Radio FiveLive. The gist was that they wanted to have a chat with me on air about the cricket and I was being given about half an hour's notice. Once again, a full day's drinking was an issue as I attempted to assemble a cogent argument on the English captaincy and just where it had all gone wrong on the tour. When the Oscars for 'Best Performance in the Field of Pretending to be Sober on Live Radio' get dished out, I'm expecting at least a nomination - if not the award itself.

After a couple of 'Were you drunk?' texts from home, it was time for me to call it a day.

I had managed to put together a formidable record, getting really bevvied on the last day of all Five Tests.

6 January

So that was that really.

The overwhelming feeling today was one of complete liberation. The nightmare scenario had happened, but at least now the suffering was over. It had, as Glennda had confidently predicted, been 5-0 after all, but at least now I could go back to being a tourist in an interesting city, rather than a 'Pommie Bastard.' At least until tonight.

In all honesty, the banter at the SCG had been fine. The Sydneysiders had been pretty magnanimous in victory, and the need to gloat was limited as the series scoreline really spoke for itself. For me, and no doubt all England fans who had followed all five Tests, that last day at Adelaide had been the killer. The writing was well and truly on the wall by then.

I had thoroughly enjoyed Perth, but my trip really had really 'jumped the shark' by the time I reached Melbourne. The derivation of this term is around TV shows, which reach a point when they ceased to be any good. The original and classic example is from *Happy Days*, when Fonzie, still wearing his leather jacket rather than a wetsuit, dons his water-skis and literally jumps a shark. Apologies if you knew all that already.

Flicking idly through the newspapers today, the most striking front page is that of the *Sydney Morning Herald*. The front page of the Sport section, which is somewhat mysteriously subtitled 'Action and Attitude', features a mock obituary, reminiscent of the very act that started The Ashes. This commemorates 'English Cricket, which died at the SCG on 5 January, 2007.'

To be fair, this is probably a really good analogy.

Watching the Melbourne and Sydney Tests was like witnessing someone in terminal decline, waiting for the final day to come. Now that day has taken place, there is a sense of relief that we can all get on with our lives, not having to tend to the ailing patient any longer.

Elsewhere in the news there was some exciting stuff around The Wiggles. Yep, you've guessed it, they are coming to the UK in 2007. I checked out the venues and there is no sign of The Cockpit in Leeds (so hot it should be called the Armpit) or the classic Empress Ballroom, Blackpool. Rumours that they are to be supported by Slipknot have yet to be substantiated.

For me personally today was about tying up a few loose ends, including the final entry on the blog, which was quite a touching moment too. In tandem with the abuse, which had been enjoyable in the most part, I had received some great support, some from people I knew and some from people I had never and would probably never meet. That's the beauty of the internet. Also, today was the day I started to look for presents to take home, which again was a pleasant feeling. I had bought a load of stuff at Steve Irwin's Zoo, which seemed like a good idea at the time, but meant that I'd had to lug it all around Australia, and to New Zealand, sweating (literally) on the baggage allowance as I went.

I'd never been away for seven weeks before and it takes a lot of getting used to. Some of us need structure in our lives to stay on the straight and narrow, one of the many things I had learned about myself is that I was indeed one of those people. I was also moving hotels for the final time, having decided to treat myself to somewhere decent for the last few nights.

A significant act was to buy myself a little something, an item that I'd thought about buying a couple of times on the trip, but hadn't got round to. It was a little self-indulgent something which might help end the trip on a really high note.

It was a ticket for the Twenty20 match against the Aussies on Tuesday night, my last evening in Australia.

Just to prove I'm a glutton's glutton for punishment, the final formal Barmy Army ceremony of the trip was to go on the 'End of Tour' cruise around Darling Harbour. This was again originally intended to be a celebratory occasion, a final nautical statement of glory as England retained The Ashes. I seriously contemplated giving it a miss, it felt more like signing up to go on some kind of Viking Funeral, burning a boat with a corpse as a spectacular tribute; the corpse of English cricket.

Having decided it would be petty not to go along, I initially revelled in quite a macabre occasion. The event that was surely intended to be a major sing-a-thon took on a different complexion. Similar to the last rites at the SCG on the previous day, after a sombre start it was quite enjoyable really. Darling Harbour is pretty impressive under lights and there is something very tranquil about cruising around the water. I managed to chat to a few interesting people, including a couple of Barmy Army organisers who'd experienced a seriously problematic tour, not helped by Cricket Australia and their prohibitive policies.

The 5-0 scoreline, which we were all helpfully reminded of by some locals from their surely exorbitantly-priced harbourside dwellings, won't have offered them much assistance either.

7 January

Another beautiful day in Sydney today, as I meandered through the busy streets and shops and just generally took it nice and easy.

The biggest dilemma today was which local football shirt to buy, a tradition I have somehow developed when visiting another land. One of the Queensland shirts was pretty smart, but despite feeling like I was over the Ashes drubbing, it was still hard to bring myself to buy anything Aussie. In the end I decided to go for the New Zealand Knights, a crap team with a dodgy kit, but at least they weren't Australian.

My thoughts had started to turn back to football, I would be back at Goodison in a week's time, and later today Everton were playing Blackburn Rovers at home in the FA Cup. My main hope was that at least they would still be in it by the time I got back. I knew t'Rovers were no great shakes, so we should be OK.

Having played poker in a super-casino and drunk out of a brown paper bag in a park, tonight I fulfilled another long-held ambition and went to an outdoor cinema. It is examples like this where you know the Aussies have got it pretty good. To be able to mooch down to a park in your shorts as the sun goes down, knowing full well than it isn't going to rain or even get at all chilly, is a good feeling.

So as I laid back with my pizza and red wine, I figured that it didn't really get much better than this. I was really looking forward to getting home, but had a feeling of serenity as my final few days in Oz were proving to be very pleasurable.

As the sun finally disappeared, certain to appear again tomorrow, the movie began. It was called *Clerks 2* and wasn't up to much to be honest. Having said that, it could have been a critically acclaimed masterpiece and I wouldn't know it. My idea of a classic film is something like Rocky IV. What do you mean it's trashy? Russia away, on Christmas Day, against a virtual robot, hard to beat.

Anyway, the movie wasn't relevant, the tranquillity of sitting back and watching a film outside was a beautiful thing. I quite like Australia now.

8 January

Time for more tourist stuff. I climbed up Sydney Harbour Bridge.

This required a really early start, but was accompanied by rubbish news from back home. I had three text messages awaiting me as I rose; all three heralded the arrival of first half Blackburn goals. Despite texting back something about going to the replay, another FA Cup run was over, before it had even started in my case.

The bridge climb set-up is run with almost military precision and must be an enormous operation. My kick-off time was half five in the morning and this was by no means the first group of the day.

Our instructor had a kind of zeal and positivity that Aussies do better than just about any other nationality. It is no coincidence that a lot of the kids TV shows are now coming out of Australia. Personally, I find myself waking up to Hi-5 on Channel Five quite a lot, but this is simply a case of watching baseball (it definitely helps you sleep) and then leaving the telly on, to be awoken by some seriously enthusiastic Aussies at 7am.

Speaking of children's TV presenters, everybody who does the climb has to wear a grey jump suit. In my case, it made me look like a presenter from some kind of cable channel for young offenders. The climb itself is exhilarating and the views it affords of Sydney are out-standing. It seems odd to think that this city isn't the capital of Australia, despite having world-famous landmarks such as the bridge and the Opera House, and even a residence for the Prime Minister.

The history of the bridge is fascinating and like so many things in Australia, hugely influenced by the British, with most of the steel coming from the North East of England. I was also interested to look at all the famous people who have done the climb before, especially loads of sporting teams, a great team building exercise no doubt. But the name that really stands out is that of American swimmer Misty Hymen. The temptation is to say that it can indeed be quite foggy on the early morning climbs, but that would be puerile. Seriously though, Mr and Mrs Hymen, I know you've had it tough, but what were you thinking?

Enough. I'm feeling completely energised by this and really loving doing the tourist thing. Shame I need to ruin my last day tomorrow with some more cricket.

9 January

So tonight it was back to the SCG for the final cricket action of the tour. England had not won any kind of game on this trip, and there were some good omens for tonight, they had greater Twenty20 experience and just maybe the shorter the game, the more even a contest it would be.

There was an excellent crowd for this abridged form of the game and Australian cricket had every reason to feel pretty pleased with itself. As I took my seat, the two blokes in front of me were especially satisfied with themselves. "I wonder if we're going to see the Poms lose for the sixth time in a row tonight," one gloat-ed to the other, clearly for my personal benefit.

"Why mate, what's been going on?" I asked. "I only got here today and haven't heard any of the results." My new friends didn't know what to make of this, bless them. I think for a lot of Australians the word irony largely passes them by. They probably think it means the same as steely:

> **Adj. Irony** – *resolute, not yielding to pressure or easily penetrating.*
>
> *E.g. The Pommie batsman showed irony determination in hitting 10 consecutive sixes. He'd make a great Aussie.*

The game started and it was clear that the Australians had left nothing to chance in terms of winding up the England fans and players. For example, situated in the seats nearest the boundary rope was a bloke with what looked like a KFC bucket on his head and a loudhailer, and he was accompanied by about a hundred people wearing similar headgear. Whenever Andrew Flintoff fielded near this group, the leader started off a chant of 5-0, 5-0, 5-0. Hats off to Freddie for laughing this off and showing an admirable amount of restraint.

The Aussies batted first and made a relatively sedate start by their standards, especially with Adam Gilchrist opening. I 'ironically' mentioned to an English lad nearby me that these Aussies are not used to this sort of cricket and don't know when they need to get on with it. Yeah right.

At the start of the sixth over, Gilchrist started going mental Perth-style and climbed into Jimmy Anderson, hitting his first three balls for six. The only relief was that he didn't go on to emulate Gary Sobers and get six sixes in one over, but by now the crowd were going mad. They were quite rightly in confident mood. As one kid near me said to his old man "Dad, will the cheer be louder than that WHEN we win?" You couldn't really fault the lad, we were less than 25% of the way through the game, but you had to fancy the Aussies already.

The carnage continued as Australia broke all kind of records and racked up a total of 221, just the 11 per over then. There was also a new kind of record being set on the row in front of me, just to my left and precisely in my eye-line when it came to watching the ball being flogged into the outfield. Part of the idea of Twenty20 was to bring youngsters and probably females along to the game of cricket. Good stuff that. However, this one particular woman starting breastfeeding her young kid when the first ball came down and he was still going for it after the innings was over. It was a pretty warm evening, but this kid was seriously thirsty. With an appetite like that he is going to grow up to be massive.

The England innings, led by Michael Vaughan making his first international appearance on the tour, started feebly and after two overs we were 10-2 and the party was pretty much over.

The gulf between the two sides was immense. England had probably two batsmen who were capable of hitting sixes, Flintoff and Pietersen, whereas all the Aussies could do it. If the batting onslaught wasn't enough, the psychological warfare continued. When Flintoff came into bat he was introduced as the 'England Captain', even though the job had been given back to Michael Vaughan. Why the Australians feel the need to be like that is mystifying really. Freddie didn't hang around too long for any more abuse, he lasted just two balls.

The least edifying sight was seeing England batsmen nurdling the ball around for singles, when the required rate was rising to 14 or 15 an over. A graphic on the scoreboard summed things up perfectly; the 'Manhattan' style chart of the two innings bore a remarkable similarity. The problem was that a different scale had to be

MANCHESTER:
THE RAINY STATE

"HOME IS NOT WHERE YOU LIVE, BUT WHERE THEY UNDERSTAND YOU."

CHRISTIAN MORGENSTERN
(GERMAN AUTHOR)

11 January - Arrive Manchester

Within 36 hours of my brief encounter of the England players kind, I was firmly back to reality in the shape of Manchester.

My Ashes dream was in tatters, but I still felt a sense of enrichment from the experience and most of all an overwhelming happiness to be home. Australia is a fascinating and in many ways spectacular place, but I'd had enough.

Just as you would expect, a January morning in Manchester was freezing cold, windy as hell and raining like mad, all at the same time. Perfect, just what I was looking for. My Australian s o j o u rn reinforced my view that I am always suspicious and usually negative about new places when I arrive. Today I was experiencing the exact antidote to that feeling, back in familiar territory and it felt great.

As the train towards my parents' house meandered past the sodden fields, I couldn't help reflecting on the land I'd left behind.

Ashes To Dust

Australia is heavily influenced by its British heritage, but as John Travolta pointed out in *Pulp Fiction*, when he told us that a Cheeseburger was known as a 'Royale with Cheese' on the continent, it's the little differences that are fascinating.

I was also thinking that maybe I'd been a bit harsh on the Aussies. They were faultless away from the subject of sport, the perfect hosts, genuinely warm in their welcome and quite rightly proud of their country. In fact, it would be fascinating to spend some time there not as a holidaymaker, but as an inmate, sorry, force of habit, an employee or even temporary resident. Just to see what it's really like. Who knows whether this is realistic? One thing I do know, I need to be there when we finally win an Ashes series down under. It's payback time then, oh yes.

One conclusion I had to draw was that cricket really matters to them. In the United Kingdom the top three sports are probably football, football and football, with cricket sharing the sidelines with rugby, tennis and athletics; occasionally hitting centre stage, but only really when big events take place. Let's face it, Henman Hill (or is it Murray Mount now?) is rammed for one week of the year tops and rugby only matters when we beat the Aussies in a World Cup final.

For the Australians it seems like international cricket is a big, big deal. Probably the one sport in which they can compete and dominate and other countries will sit up and take notice. Yeah, I know they're good at swimming, but away from the Olympics, that's pretty low profile on the world stage.

Maybe their reaction and pure determination to blast England away on and off the pitch is borne out of this zeal to be the best team in the world at cricket, which they have been for ages, and to avenge any defeats spectacularly. The reception that awaited the visiting fans at Brisbane was pretty unpleasant, but things certainly improved as the tour progressed. Maybe it is the sort of reaction a visiting football team would get over here.

As my train broke down just before the penultimate station of my journey, round the back of some grimy old industrial units, no-one was too bothered. It was definitely a cold day, just maybe the train didn't fancy it. It certainly didn't perturb me, I was still pleased to be home. There was a little less to think about here.

There was absolutely no chance of any bush fires in the fields around Kirkham that day. Anyone wearing thongs would have them well tucked away and certainly wouldn't dream of putting them on their feet. There wasn't a clever or evocative name, like the Freemantle Doctor, for the wind either. It was more of a wet nurse.

And even if we had a hole in the ozone layer above us, the thick and dark clouds would pose an impenetrable barrier. Factor 30 plus was already a distant dream and if I had the inclination, I could go from one major city to another in less than an hour without having to go through the ordeal of using an airport, which suited me fine. Once the train had got going anyway.

So the trip of a lifetime had proved to be just that, even though the cricket had been a major letdown. Talisman Freddie Flintoff really hadn't proved to be the ideal captaincy candidate after all and the spirit of Ashes 2005 had been ruthlessly destroyed. It took England 16 years to win the Ashes and just 15 days to lose them again.

But not to worry, at least I could say one thing:

I was there.

11 February

One month on and it feels like I've been back for ages.

Catching up with people I haven't seen for a while is strange, you see not that much happens in a normal couple of months, it just feels like I've been away for so much longer.

The day after I made it back onto English soil there was a cricket match to watch. Yep, the one-dayers had started and it was England against Australia. Having amassed a decent total, the visitors were comprehensively outplayed as the Aussies cruised to an easy victory. How did I feel?

A maelstrom of emotions was at play, but despite being disappointed by the result I felt a weird sense of relief too. It would have felt a bit unfair if they won the first game after I'd got back, especially as they hadn't really threatened to win anything while I was there. No blahddy warries on that score though, the Aussies were just far too good.

The next sport I watched was to see Everton play Reading at Goodison, a game significant for the presence of three American goalkeepers, Marcus Hahnemann, Tim Howard and the visiting Sylvester Stallone, in town to promote *Rocky 54* or whatever number he's up to. I was worried that the normally sceptical home fans would give him a tough time, but he was greeted pretty enthusiastically really. Thankfully, the club resisted the temptation to hold a minute's silence for Apollo Creed.

Once the game started it felt wholly ironic to hear the Reading fans singing "Barmy Army" and "Your support is facking shit" and loads of other classics. They were witless attempts compared to some of the England fans efforts in Australia, but if felt odd to be on the receiving end once again. I saw a couple of lads I'd watched the Chelsea match with in the Burswood Casino in Perth, which just made the day seem even more surreal. Small world and all that.

The day after the Reading game I started my new job and this involves a tortuous journey along the M62, traversing the Pennines with countless others. This was probably the final act of getting back to normality. Going away for a few weeks helps you realise quite a lot about yourself and in my case, having a job keeps me sane. Having to work for a living did mean that it wasn't that easy for me to keep up to date with the cricket, but this seemed like a blessing of sorts.

As the Commonwealth Bank Series rumbled forward it was more obvious than ever. Australia were streets ahead of England and New Zealand, both of whom were playing for second place. And it looked alarmingly like the Kiwis would claim that spot as well.

I couldn't help chuckling to myself when I read debutant Mal Loye's comment about his first game for England at the GABBA. When asked if the Aussie fielders had given him any grief, he said that everything was cool in the middle. The crowd was a different story though. "I've never been abused like that in my life," he said. "I thought I was a reasonable bloke until yesterday!" I know what you mean, Mal.

Now I may well have experienced a nightmare before Christmas and it didn't get much better around New Year. But towards the end of January, we witnessed a miracle. The magical occurrence appeared to be linked to comments by none other than Australian coach John Buchanan. Yes, the man who makes Pauline Fowler seem like a laugh a minute indulged in that famous Aussie trait, just getting a little bit too cocky.

Late in January 2007, in his typically professorial way he said "In essence, the batting efforts of our opposition are not assisting the development of our bowlers' one-day skills, and the decision-making that accompanies being placed under the microscope of competition." Roughly translated this means "You're shit and you know you are."

Deliciously, this comment preceeded England's first victory over Australia on the tour, and a complete volte-face in the fortunes of the two countries. There were two games remaining and both had to go the right way for England to reach the finals. The next and most bizarre feeling was to support the Aussies (I felt so dirty) against New Zealand, whom they duly despatched and then

213

England had to beat the Kiwis.

As most people will know this game went our way and was followed quickly by a seemingly inevitable convincing England victory in the first final.

Me and my Ashes buddy Matt had decided we would watch at least one of the games together, but never really envisaged it would be the potentially deciding game of the final series with England 1-0 up. As it started at 3am I told him that I'd head over to his gaff for the second innings. England posted a decent total despite the best efforts of Glenn McGrath, who managed to get a wicket with his last ball of international cricket in Australia.

Typical.

That said the target England set the now increasingly fragile Aussies was pretty competitive.

And they got nowhere near it. Fearing the worst, I still had a couple of moments when I thought they could still do it, but in all honesty England were always in control. England had batted really well, maybe even assisting the development of the Australian bowlers' one day skills and the decision-making that accompanies being placed under the microscope of competition, you might say.

If England's batsmen were good, their bowlers were irresistible. Australia were soon 56-5 as Hayden, Ponting, Gilchrist, Clarke and Hussey went in quick succession. Having watched this lot bat for interminable periods during The Ashes, it was great to see them almost trip over each other as they made their way to and from the pavilion.

Having looked like tortured, troubled and haunted souls throughout The Ashes, the England players suddenly looked happy to be there, revelling in their success.

The end, when it came, didn't go exactly to plan. Glenn McGrath, having presumably borrowed Warnie's scriptwriter now he didn't need it, managed to make it rain so that he wouldn't have to go out and bat to face the final indignity of defeat. England won by 34 runs, but that was a landslide really.

This time it was the Aussies' turn to trudge over to the England players and offer handshakes, through somewhat gritted teeth. Pleasingly, not one of them managed to look as unhappy in defeat as Prime Minister John Howard at the 2003 Rugby World Cup. The PM had the appearance of someone who just had a little bit of dog shite stuck right under his nose as he handed the winners' medals to the victorious England side that day.

Well, we won that day and we managed it again in the one-day series.

Matt and I raised a glass of Coopers, he's still got a taste for it you know, and toasted England success. The ghost of Day 5 in Adelaide could finally be laid to rest. And there was no need to worry about Aussies until the World Cup.

This wasn't exactly August 2005 with tickertape glistening in the sunshine at the Oval. For me, it was a chilly February morning in Yorkshire, with the odd carrier bag being carried on the breeze through a gloomy, windswept landscape. But we won.

Now we can look forward to the Ashes 2009 and hope that the rumours are indeed true that a Japanese firm has developed a camera with a shutter speed so fast, it can actually catch an Aussie with his mouth shut.

Ashes To Dust

Appendices

Best supported football teams amongst the Barmy Army
1. Man City
2. Everton
3. Sunderland
4. Portsmouth
5. West Brom
6. Sheffield Wednesday
7. Liverpool
8. Spurs
9. Crystal Palace
10. Blackpool

Best cricket grounds to visit
1. Adelaide
2. Perth
3. Melbourne
4. Brisbane
5. Sydney

Best cities to vist
1. Perth
2. Sydney
3. Brisbane
4. Adelaide
5. Melbourne

Top non-cricket news stories
1. The Wiggles
2. The Bush fires
3. Ian Thorpe
4. Coup in Fiji (pronounced foy-joy)
5. Police mistreatment of aboriginals
6. New Year's Eve

Best blog insults
1. Big-mouthed slob
2. Uncultured moron
3. Disgrace to your country
4. Bigoted loudmouth
5. Slack-jawed yokel
6. Captain Moron
7. Big-mouthed girl
8. Dopey bastard
9. Inbred moron
10. Dickspank Pommie c***

Potential England Ashes XI for 2009
1. Andrew Strauss
2. Alistair Cook
3. Ian Bell
4. Kevin Pietersen
5. Paul Collingwood
6. Andrew Flintoff
7. Steven Davies
8. Stuart Broad
9. Monty Panesar
10. Simon Jones
11. Sajid Mahmood

Potential Australia Ashes XI for 2009

1. Phil Jaques
2. Chris Rogers
3. Ricky Ponting
4. Adam Voges
5. Shane Watson
6. Andrew Symonds
7. Brad Haddin
8. Mitchell Johnson
9. Stuart Clark
10. Dan Cullen
11. Ben Hilfenhaus

A-League players British fans may recognise

1. Carl Veart
2. Bobby Petta
3. Tony Vidmar
4. Sean Devine
5. Scott Gemmill
6. Neil Emblen
7. Steve Corica
8. Simon Lynch
9. Paul Okon
10. Stan Lazaridis
11. Danny Allsop
12. Grant Brebner
13. Kevin Muscat

Coach: Terry Butcher

Real records broken during the tour

5-0   Second whitewash in Ashes history - Australia

14   Most sixes in a Twenty20 Innings - Australia

100 off 57 balls   Adam Gilchrist
        second quickest Test century ever

209   Ricky Ponting and Mike Hussey
        Highest 2nd wicket partnership at Brisbane

221-5   Australia
        Highest ever total in International Twenty20

602-9 declared   Australia
        Second highest Ashes total at Brisbane

700 Test wickets   Shane Warne

900 International wickets   Glenn McGrath

1,000 International wickets   Shane Warne

Alternative records

5,902   Australian fielders' shouts of "Catch it"

5,681   Australian fielders' shouts of "Catch it" as the
ball rolls along the ground

903   Aussie cricketers starting an interview answer
with 'Look'

Appendices

812 Aussie cricketers starting an interview answer with 'Aw'

604 Aussie cricketers starting an interview answer with 'Jeez'

394 Aussie cricketers starting an interview answer with 'Aw, Jeez, Look'

247 Aussie fans talking their way into getting thrown out

102 Times *God Save Your Queen* sung by the Barmy Army

76 Separate occasions the Aussie media moaned about Totti's penalty in the World Cup

41 Conversations in which Australians said 'football', but meant something else

5 Australian Test grounds that will let Billy and his trumpet in if we don't hold the Ashes next time

Ashes To Dust

Ashes To Dust

Ashes To Dust